I Didn't Mean For This To Happen

How To Repair Your Life And Marriage After Trust Has Been Broken

Cathy Patterson-Sterling

Copyright © 2012 Cathy Patterson-Sterling
All rights reserved.

ISBN: 1-4776-9127-8
ISBN-13: 9781477691274

Contents

Introduction: Containing The Emotional Accident Scene
Chapter One: What Just Happened? — 1
Chapter Two: How Did We Get Here? — 21
Chapter Three: Now What? Can Broken Trust Be Healed? — 93
Chapter Four: How Do We Move Forward? — 113
Chapter Five: Releasing Ourselves From
    The Shadow Of The Past — 125
Chapter Six: The Potential Of Your Relationship — 131
Chapter Seven: Stepping Into God's Larger Story — 139
Chapter Eight: Live The Choice Now! — 147

Introduction: Containing The Emotional Accident Scene

As Lynda arrived home, she sunk gently into her soft leather chair as she reached over to press the circular button attached to the front of her computer tower. She rubbed her eyes wearily and stretched from her long day at work. Suddenly a message intercepted the middle of the screen with a quick flash. The next second became a moment frozen in time that would change the entire course of her life. The message provided her with a doorway into a world-a secret world- of lies and deceit that would shake the foundation of her soul and her marriage forever. Lynda's husband had been lying to her and he had built up a secret escape world of sexting, cybersex, and pornography to which Lynda had no idea about whatsoever until now. She felt as if her world was about to tumble down into a solid crash!

Lynda's experience is not uncommon in a society whereby anonymity, fantasy, and temptation can be satisfied with the click of a button. More and more Christian couples are having the "I Didn't Mean For This To Happen" conversation which is a crisis in their marriages when one person has created an emotional mess by acting-out with pornography, having inappropriate sexual conversations in any form or through texts (sexting), engaging in emotional affairs by having intimate or private talks of a seductive nature outside of the marriage, or with compulsively spending money with online shopping and so on. Since we live in a social media world whereby we leave electronic footprints through our virtual voyages into forbidden lands, the chances of getting caught with our actions are instant as well as immediate unless of course we believe we have the knowledge to cover up these footprints which then leads to living a double life. The danger of course is that sin thrives in the secrecy of shadows. As Christians we may be lured by the secrecy and anonymity we believe we have, only to then discover that our actions are revealed through the very technology we think we can escape within. Broken trust occurs when we are lured into the shadows of sin and our actions are exposed before our partners who now do not trust us.

The unity of the Christian marriage can become entangled in a web of lies particularly if one partner strays into the world of sexual sin, instant gratification, or chemical indulgence. Lies, affairs, internet sex, and addictions can easily serve as vehicles of tremendous deception that leave the other partner in the marriage trying to fill a gaping hole in their wounded souls pierced by betrayal. Sexual sin is not the only culprit of tearing down the trust factor in marriages. Couples can also be impacted by compulsive spending of money or any type of activity that is protected in secrecy and coated in lies. All deceptions related to activities such as pornography, emotional affairs, physical affairs, cybersex, compulsive spending of money/shopping, compulsive on-line gaming, problem gambling, and so on all have one thing in common which is an emotional accident scene at the center of people's marriages because trust has become shattered in some way.

Lynda's Emotional Accident Scene

In the above story, Lynda became involved in an emotional accident scene with her husband. She felt emotionally blindsided as she *collided* with her husband's secret world of lies as well as deceptions. Lynda confronted her husband about his sexual sin and he eventually admitted to having issues with pornography and acting-out sexually through sexting as well as contacting all kinds of women as they had "cybersex" (talking about their sexual fantasies) with each other over the internet. At that point Lynda felt the overwhelming emotional waves of humiliation, fear, as well as rage particularly since Lynda and her husband served as a worship ministry couple and had many people in the congregation "watching their actions" as they were unofficial role-models as a young married couple in leadership in their church. They were even contemplating moving over to the youth ministry to lead the youth as her husband had plans to train as a youth pastor. Now Lynda felt like she was on a collision course with her own husband who was supposed to be one of her greatest supporters as well as closest people in her life. Essentially, Lynda felt "tossed under the bus" as if her husband had been so selfish as well as reckless that he didn't care about her feelings or what his actions would do to their relationship. She knew she didn't want a divorce, but the lies as well as deceits felt like an insurmountable mountain to climb in her life as she wondered where to even start in this process?

When There Is An Emotional Accident Scene In Your Marriage

If you are reading this book then chances are that you woke up one day and life as you knew it had changed completely. Your sense of innocence as well as security had been altered or possibly even shattered as you received news in some form that would threaten the level of trust at the center of your relationships. Your partner lied and appeared to be "protecting something." Likely, you felt like your best interests were not even considered and you are worried about what the future holds. Will you get more of the same behaviour again later on? You may even wonder what you are dealing with because sorting out the truth of what is happening may feel like trying to get blood out of a stone as you spin around in circles sorting your way through the murky deceptions around you in your relationships. At some level you may even not only fear the future, but also worry if what you are feeling is even real? Many people in these situations know at an intuitive level that something is very wrong, however, they have a fear that they are over-reacting as they try to even understand or make sense of the issues before them. Then there are many individuals who begin a self-esteem spiral as they worry that there is something wrong with themselves that has "caused" their spouses to act-out, lie, as well as deceive. All of these feelings are normal along a journey that feels very much like an emotional rollercoaster. Just when people sense they are "on top" or are getting a grip on their issues, there is another curve or turn in the process.

You may have discovered that your spouse had a porn problem, an affair, or trust was broken in some way. There is now damage and you are wondering what to do next as you likely feel that you are in some way emotionally drowning in fear as well as panic. Your spouse may look at you and say: "I didn't mean for this to happen!" The problem is that an apology in many ways can feel empty or fruitless because this does not feel like a minor hiccup on the course of a long, healthy, and sustaining marriage. Instead, with the degree of lies as well as deceptions the future may even look quite uncertain or even in some ways dim. Sorry does not take the pain away and an acknowledgement that this should not have happened is not always helpful because the reality is that it did happen and may even still be occurring now!

An emotional earthquake has sounded and there is a cataclysmic fracture or fault line that has shot through the very center of your relationship. What you thought was life and all that was closest to you is now impacted by this facture line and you are left starring with disbelief at the wreckage of this scene. Some people have further "aftershocks" as their partners reveal later even more details about a hidden "escape life" or side of themselves which was a secret world whereby they acted-out sexually, spent money compulsively, were using drugs/alcohol to numb their minds, or they spun a web of deceitful lies in some manner.

Your Story

This book is your emotional compass as well as map for a healing journey that you are starting so that you can reclaim your life from fear, negativity, and the damage of broken trust. You can grow on deeper emotional as well as spiritual levels and actually come out of these circumstances an even stronger person who is better for going through these situations. Likely, we would not wish these problems on our worst enemies but we can take what is given to us and grow in a deeper walk with God while also using these problems as a time of transformation to grow into the larger design of God's plan for our lives. God does not waste a good crisis and there are greater reasons why we walk through the adversity that we do in life. This is all part of a larger journey.

Everybody has a different story so the degree of shock you feel and the circumstances in which you came to understand the nature of the broken trust in your relationship is all very different. For many individuals this was a dramatic scene while for some people the trust just eroded over time as their work-addicted spouses were emotionally unavailable and rarely home due to all of their working. The result is a long time erosion of broken trust in which the spouse feels that their partner "chose" work over them and that they cannot trust them to meet their emotional needs. Then with this already existing emotional gap in the relationship, a work-addicted spouse may have compulsively spent money, engaged in an affair, and so on. This broken trust occurs in such relationships whereby trust has not only been fractured but has eroded the core of any good will in the marriage. Therefore the recent events may be just another pile of issues added to an already fragile relationship. Everyone has their own unique situations but what we all have in common is that the reaction to broken trust in our relationships is multi-layered with various feelings. Part of the journey is to feel our feelings and to work through this grief as well as loss because the innocence from our relationships has been claimed. There is an emotional cost that comes with the breaking of trust. In the long run, we can use this immense pain towards our own personal transformation as we grow from these experiences.

This is a book for people having the "*I didn't mean for this to happen*" conversation in their marriages because they are dealing with the issue of broken trust. Readers may be the "*acting-out party*" who broke the trust with their deceptions or they may be the "*hurting party*" which are the individuals on the receiving end of the lies. This crisis of trust is often a confusing time and in this book readers will learn how long buried emotional issues rise to the surface of relationships and why acting-out occurs along with the resulting lies as well as deceptions. Furthermore, readers will learn about the steps of the recovery as well as healing journeys involved in repairing these relationships. Even when the foundation of trust in a relationship is fractured, there is an opportunity to rebuild if the proper steps as well as measures are put into place. This is a challenging journey but a soul-fulfilling one as people learn how to peel back the layers of who they are to rebuild as well as transform into the potential of who they are individually as they work on their emotional issues along with who they are collectively as a couple in the greatest potential of their relationships. God is the miracle worker and through adversity there is the possibility of transformation as we grow through our crisis into the larger design of who God wants us to be. We can be like the silver that is tempered as well as refined through the fire except that our tempering happens with affliction (Isaiah 48:10). We are changed by these experiences but such transformations can be positive as we step up to who God has called us to be or the alternative is to spiral in anger as well as bitterness.

My name is Cathy Patterson-Sterling and I am a Christian Counsellor who has walked alongside thousands of people through the last fourteen years during their darkest moments through addiction as well as the crisis of broken trust. In our Christian communities there is often a veil of secrecy and you would be surprised by the numbers of people who have been impacted by broken trust with pornography, lusting, emotional affairs, compulsive spending of money and other lies as well as deceptions. Every client or couple I counsel serve as a beacon of light as they courageously walk this journey of picking up the pieces shattered by broken trust while reclaiming back their lives and often their marriages. With their powerful testimonies, they give permission for others to share their stories. In our technological age with the ability to be part of a global community and with such access to information at the click of our fingers on computers, this problem of sexual sin and broken trust is increasing rapidly. We will examine the reasons why deception is taking hold of relationships and walk together in the magnificent journey of healing that can result in amazing fruit of strength, courage, and resiliency as we grow on deeper emotional as well as spiritual levels as a result of surviving as well as healing from this crisis in our lives.

Ephesians 3:20

"Now to him who is able to do immeasurably more than all we ask or imagine, according to his power that is at work within us,"

Chapter 1
What Just Happened?

Sylvia stood before her husband with her hands trembling in upset. Her head was pounding and she was on the verge of passing out if it was not for the nausea that churned in her stomach. She was so conflicted inside because part of her wanted to scream with a consuming rage and the other side of her wanted a hug from her husband as assurance that this awful moment would just go away. The problem was that the husband that stood before Sylvia was the same man trying to spin a myriad of lies as well as justifications as to why he had been spending so much time secretly lusting after her best friend. Just when Sylvia had thought she had enough of this horrible moment, her husband looked at her to say: "I never meant for this to happen. I am confused and I am not sure if I am still in love with you."

Sylvia was in an emotional car accident scene with her husband and she felt completely blind-sided. She was trying to process what was happening in front of her when the *emotional bomb* was dropped in that her husband who thought he was being honest shared that he was attracted to another woman (Sylvia's best friend) and that he was confused about his feelings for her in this marriage. That evening Sylvia sobbed uncontrollably as she felt like her world was falling apart. The next day Sylvia's husband declared that he had "come to this senses" as he begged for her forgiveness and said that he was just going crazy or having a crisis of some kind. He was dedicated to rebuilding their relationship back together again and he wanted to salvage their family as well as be there for Sylvia and their three young children.

Even though Sylvia and her husband agreed that they would "work" on their relationship, Sylvia was left with the feeling of impending dread that rested in the pit of her stomach. Not all was well in her world and she felt as if she was "walking on emotional eggshells" wondering if her husband would stray from their marriage not just emotionally as he had done but physically as well? In many ways Sylvia felt like a hostage in her own marriage bracing for some kind of future fall-out around what her husband would or would not do next. Sylvia loved her husband, but she could not trust the circumstances. He had gone outside of their marriage to meet his emotional needs and she feared that it would be just a matter of time before he started acting-out sexually out of the relationship with other women as well. Sylvia was experiencing extreme emotional abandonment worrying that the man she had signed up to be with in life was the same person "tossing her under the bus" by recklessly pursuing other women outside of their marriage. Sylvia experienced a multitude of feelings that came in layers as she worried about the security of her future. Before she could even allow herself to feel those deeper fears, she had to even process what was happening. Essentially, Sylvia was in shock.

The Shock After The Emotional Collision

If you have experienced broken trust, the most normal initial reaction is one of shock. You are presented with information or evidence which indicates that life as you know it is not the same. There are lies or deceptions and a secret world of some kind purposefully being hidden from you by someone else.

In order to process this information, most people go into *shock*. They feel numb on an emotional level as well as nauseous on a physical level. Many of my clients will describe how they feel like this is a "sick joke" in which they believe people are going to call out "surprise" because they are really on a secret reality show, candid camera, or a bad television episode of "Punked." Unfortunately, they are not stars in a television show and instead they are living a real life crisis as they come to terms with what is even happening before them. As days go by and they begin to process or understand this alternate reality and what this information means, they often feel like they are adjusting to a "new normal" in which life is different. Such people have lost their innocence and are instead seeing things in their life with a new set of emotional glasses in which they are experiencing tremendous pain. Hurting parties are left picking up the pieces of shattered dreams as they adjust to a new sense of how things will be now that they know about the deceptions and the capability of their spouses around lying as well as spinning webs of deceit. Many hurting parties feel lost as well as confused as they try and rectify the image of who they married versus the reality of the lies as well as deceits before them now.

An Emotional Train-Wreck

The reality is that acting-out parties who break trust likely do not wake up one day deciding that they would like to cause their partners an immense amount of pain. Instead, such people are dealing with their own unresolved emotional issues that are rising to the surface of their relationships. Such issues may have been long buried, but in marriage they are activated once again. The pornography, emotional affairs, lusting, sexual sins, compulsive spending of money and so on that are shrouded in layers of lies as well as secrecy are symptomatic of deeper issues that have never been addressed. Therefore there is not only an emotional accident scene but there is an emotional train that has been in motion for a long time. Now that emotional train has "hit a wall" with the acting-out behaviour and the ensuing broken trust. There is metal as well as debris everywhere and these issues can no longer be ignored.

Self-destructive behaviour that damages relationships is driven by something and does not come out of nowhere. People who act deceitful in their relationships and are prepared to lie are protecting something so underneath there are unresolved emotional issues. With the crisis of broken trust, there is an ability to work through the longstanding, buried issues that were never dealt with over the years. Many people come to their marriages with these issues and through the crisis of broken trust, they can no longer ignore the percolating problems underneath the surface of their relationships. In Sylvia's story, her husband was a person who never dealt with issues. He was a people-pleaser that worked long hours and he had lost himself in building up a life filled with responsibilities as he tried to support his family. As he stuffed his feelings he battled with depression as he internalized everything that went on his life and never dealt with deeper emotions. Therefore when Sylvia's best friend showed him attention as well as admiration, his ego was "ripe for the picking" because an infatuation with her was the perfect distraction he thought in which he could escape from the burden of responsibilities and all the mounting pressures as well as piling up issues that he never dealt with in his life. Now that Sylvia and her husband had encountered this emotional train-wreck in their marriage, they could address these deeper problems and work through their communication. Sylvia's husband could no longer deny his feelings and ignore issues because this emotional way of dealing with life had cracks with him being vulnerable to his ego as well as lusting as an escape from his real issues. While participating in a recovery journey, Sylvia's husband looked at how

I Didn't Mean For This To Happen

he became susceptible to temptation and lusting. As a result, he could see how he stepped away from God's standard as well as call to who is he is supposed to be as a husband, father, and Christian.

So people who break trust and act-out have an opportunity to really unpack what is driving their issues by doing the necessary work as part of a *recovery journey*. Now for hurting parties, they have the challenge of processing their feelings which are all within a multitude of layers. These feelings may start with initial shock, then anger, hurt, sadness, and feelings of emotional abandonment. Imagine a pyramid with shock being at the highest point and underneath that shock is anger as well as all of the deeper feelings. The challenge for hurting parties is to work through these layers so that they do not experience a sensation of just rushing forward towards forgiveness only to feel haunted by fear that these experiences of broken trust will surface again in their relationships. If hurting parties work through their feelings, then they can begin healing as they gain a sense of understanding as well as closure. As a result, they can move through these feelings and then achieve a sense of forgiveness as well as freedom from the past. Such people are able to come to terms with what has happened, feel the feelings, move through their experiences, and then move on without being pulled back into the grip of the past.

Grief

Hurting parties dealing with broken trust are having to move through feelings of grief. With grief, we are mourning a loss. As people we deal with grief when life is suddenly interrupted. For example, life as we knew it with all of our routines as well as predictability has been altered. With this new information around the broken trust, we have lost our innocence and have to process what these new details mean for us, our relationships, and our futures. Also, many hurting parties have to reconcile the images of who they thought they married, the life they signed up for in marriage, and the reality of what they are dealing with now with the broken trust. Therefore many hurting parties feel like their illusions as well as sense of securities in their marriages has been shattered. Life is not the same as there has been betrayal on some level. Likely, acting-out parties have lied and appear to be "protecting something." As a result hurting parties have to reconcile how their partners who are supposed to be their greatest supporters appeared to "switch teams" and work against them through the lies as well as deceits. Therefore many hurting parties end up experiencing grief as they mourn the loss of innocence in their relationships.

Hurting parties have the challenge of dealing with the new information around the broken trust as they come to terms with what this new knowledge means for their relationships. As they pick up the shattered pieces from the emotional train wreck, they also have an opportunity to rebuild their relationship from the foundation upwards. In order to rebuild, hurting parties need to first process their feelings and do the journey of walking through the impact of the acting-out behaviours as well as the broken trust.

Moving Through The Tunnel Of Feelings

As in the example with Sylvia, once the shock wears off, rage is the most common feeling that spouses experience when their partners have lied or acted in a deceptive manner. In many cases, deceived spouses feel a deep sense of betrayal because the dreams and hopes for the future that they shared with their partners are under attack. The partners they thought who were working alongside of them to build a life together appear to switch teams and have become potential enemies. Therefore deceived spouses often feel very conflicted because they are balancing feelings of love as well as anger at the same time and do not know if they can trust that their partners will not act without integrity again. As a result such betrayed spouses are now lost in an emotional vacuum wondering if they should continue loving their partners or put their energies into protecting themselves from the potential for further deceit.

In most instances, deceived spouses have legitimate anger because their partners who they love as well as treasure have engaged in some type of actions that threaten, undermine, or even lessen the value of the soul bond of marriage. The reactions of spouses who are lied to or deceived run along a continuum whereby trust may be broken or even shattered. Also there are situations whereby spouses did not just lie but engaged in activities that have resulted in a major betrayal or violation of the marriage vow because they were adulterous or even scandalous. The important point is to not measure the varying severity of behaviours, but instead to focus more on the pain of deceived spouses. One of the biggest stumbling blocks to healing is the unresolved resentments that can set in marriages so that even if the relationship is salvageable, deceived spouses can find it difficult to move forward because they are still angry as well as fearful that such deceits can potentially occur again.

The emotions that deceived spouses often feel are a necessary part of the healing process. Often people's reactions to broken trust form a pattern whereby they experience a repetition of familiar feelings and just keep cycling through these same emotions. Initially, this emotional cycle is helpful because individuals need to feel the shock, vulnerability, powerlessness, sadness, anger, as well as hurt so they can come to terms with the events that have occurred in their marriages. Such feelings are normal and these emotions become part of a familiar cycle which we will refer to as a tunnel of feelings. There is no instant relief for these feelings of upset immediately, but it is important to express these emotions as a way of processing or coming to terms with situations in which trust is broken. Also there is a light at the end of the tunnel and the challenge is to just keep moving forward through these feelings.

Now all people are individuals and they can deal with broken trust in their marriages in different ways. When trust is broken in marriages, the first reaction of spouses who have been deceived experience is shock and then a sense of being vulnerable or devastated as well as feeling stripped of everything. This sense of being overwhelmed can be expressed as vulnerability. Finally, deceived spouses often justifiably feel like victims as something "was done to them" or that they were unduly wronged. After feeling like a victim, some spouses who are betrayed will feel martyrdom in that they focus on all of their good actions or sacrifices they have made for their marriages. In the martyrdom phase, deceived spouses feel an overwhelming sense of life being unfair especially since they have been so loving in their marriages and yet their partners have acted without integrity by lying or being deceptive. After experiencing this sense of unfairness in the relationship, deceived spouses will often then experience anger which then leads to feelings of vulnerability, emotional abandonment, and hurt. Now let's examine these common reactions in the tunnel of feelings in more detail.

Shock

Some deceived spouses are aware of their partners' lies and deceptions but they hope that these actions will not have a negative impact on their marriages. In other words, the spouses who are betrayed acknowledge the issues in their relationships but they just pray that things will get better or go away completely. For example, Julia notices that every time she walks into the den of

I Didn't Mean For This To Happen

her house that her husband almost jumps out of his chair and flaps his arms about wildly to change screens on his computer. He talks a lot about the chat rooms he visits and how the people he talks to all around the world are very interesting. In particular, he mentions a lady in Singapore that he speaks with who is absolutely fascinating. Julia dismisses her husband's comments as a passing phase and believes that he is just excited about the technological capabilities of his new computer system and how interactive he can be with people from around the world with this fast speed processing component which makes his computer run that much more smoothly.

At some point Julia opens up the computer and receives a pop-up instant message from a lady named Sulay wondering if her husband will be leaving this week or next on his flight to Singapore. Julia goes into a state of shock upon learning that her husband has been deceiving her and that his interactions with this woman have been far from innocent. In this phase of shock, Julia is trying to understand the full ramifications of her husband's actions. He has been dishonest and something bad has happened. Julia is overwhelmed and her reaction is just plain shock as she feels emotionally immobilized as well as numb. The predominant thought for Julia is: "What just happened?" Events now are dramatically different than they were ten seconds ago before she received this message.

The following includes some common characteristics of shock. In this phase of shock people may experience these possibilities.

The Experience of Shock:
- Surprise upon discovering a detail or action that is deceitful.

- Sensation of feeling completely overwhelmed by realizing that there are ramifications and that reality as you see it is somehow very different than it was even seconds earlier before discovering this deceitful event or action.
- Trying to come to terms with the deceitful detail or action before you and feeling a sensation of stomach upset, numbness, and increase in heart rate.
- Feeling overwhelmed and wondering how the person you love could have been so deceitful? You may even wish desperately for an excuse that will make this bad situation go away or wonder if maybe the evidence before you is really a misunderstanding or mistake.
- Experiencing numbness as well as a sensation of fear as well as shortness of breath.
- On an emotional level feeling frozen, paralyzed, or numb. This experience is similar to falling and hurting yourself. The body goes into shock before the healing can begin. For example, a person who falls may feel numb with pain and then the body goes into swelling around the wounded area to compensate for the injury. If you have been deceived, you may just feel frozen in fear before coming to terms with the deceitful actions.

Vulnerable/ Devastated / Feeling Stripped of Everything

While still feeling the shock of coming to terms with deceitful events, some spouses experience vulnerability. At this point they feel "caught off guard" or wounded as part of an overall sensation of being vulnerable, feeling devastated or having a sense that they have been stripped of everything. This is the phase when deceived spouses feel the pain of realizing that the partners they care and love for have been working against them and have acted

I Didn't Mean For This To Happen

with a lack of integrity. Some betrayed spouses may feel duped as if they have taken the first hit in a battle that they were not even aware that they were having to endure. This experience is similar to being punched by someone without even being aware that the person doing the hitting was mad or even capable of assault in the first place. The assault in this metaphor seemed to come out of nowhere similar to a "sucker punch" with the person on the receiving end feeling susceptible or vulnerable.

As in the above example, Julia feels wounded as well as vulnerable and devastated because she was not aware that her husband was emotionally involved with another woman from Singapore on the internet. The man she married stood in integrity as well as honour. Furthermore, he is an Elder in the church and is highly respected by other people. Julia feels betrayed as well as unprotected. She is forced to face the consequences of her husband's deceit with no support at all. The man who is supposed to comfort her is now her opponent in a battle that she never saw brewing on the horizon.

The Experience of Being Vulnerable and Devastated:
- Reeling from an experience of deceit
- Feeling of being under attack and not being prepared
- Coming to terms with the fact that I am under attack
- Sensation of being wounded and susceptible to even more pain
- Feeling bare as well as unsupported. This sensation is similar to the experience of being thrown into battle with no ammunition and forced to fight a loved one who has become a foe or armed adversary.

Powerless

While feeling vulnerable, many deceived spouses will then start to experience a sensation of being powerless. In essence, they are overwhelmed with the onslaught of personal questions that they have that have arose out of their experiences of being deceived. Some common questions from partners who have been lied to or deceived include: What does this deceit mean for our marriage? Can we fix this situation and just make the pain go away? What do I do? What about our children and the future that we have built together? If my partner has lied now, will he/she do it again? Can we still live together? How can I be strong and how can we get through this? In this phase, deceived partners consider all of these questions and possibly more as they feel an overwhelming sense of powerlessness because they are not in a state to make any major decisions.

In the example with Julia, after she experiences the initial sensation of being wounded and feeling vulnerable, she becomes overwhelmed considering the implications of her husband's behaviour as well as the impact on their marriage. She is still unclear also as to how she will confront her husband and if he is really planning on leaving their marriage and going to Singapore? While considering all of these questions as well as possibilities, Julia feels powerless as well as overwhelmed.

In situations whereby emotional infidelity is not an issue, deceived spouses can still experience this sense of powerlessness as they consider the implications that their partners' lies or deceitful actions have on their marriages. Even if a spouse is abusing alcohol or drugs, deceived partners at this stage are coming to terms with the fact that the drinking or drugging behaviours are just getting worse and that some type of action or response will be needed.

The Experience Of Being Powerless:
- Feeling overwhelmed in an attempt to consider a number of questions around how the deceit could have hap-

I Didn't Mean For This To Happen

pened and what these dishonourable actions mean in terms of the future of the marriage.
- Being consumed in the questions of "What" or "How" this deceitful situation could have occurred and then feeling powerless to intervene or change the course of events. Therefore you are still trying to come to terms with the deceitful actions that have occurred.

Victim/ Feeling "Done To"

Once betrayed spouses start to understand the exact nature of the deceit (the "what" and "how" of what happened), then they may feel the heaviness of being wronged. In the victim phase of the tunnel of feelings, spouses who have been deceived by their partners feel "done to" as they focus on the adversity or challenges that lay ahead in the marriage rebuilding process if their relationships does survive the betrayal. A common reaction is for deceived spouses to say: "This is not what I signed up for when I got married." As a result, such partners on the receiving end of deceit feel the impact of the betrayal as they recognize how they have been lied to as well as deceived. Such deceived partners thought that life was a certain way until they realized the extent of their loved one's lies and/or manipulations. Many spouses who have been betrayed often feel like victims of an emotional car accident in which (on a metaphorical level) they were driving along only to be suddenly T-Boned by a reckless driver who was completely inconsiderate of their space or place on the roadway.

In Julia's example, she enters the victim phase of healing by realizing the nature of her husband's wrongs. He had pretended to be a loving as well as devoted husband except that his real attention as well as energy was towards a budding emotional relationship that was occurring over the internet. In this circumstance, Julia "feels done to and unduly wronged" (like a victim) because she was holding up her end of the marriage by being a faithful as well as loving wife.

The Experience Of Being A Victim:
- Focusing on the details of the deceitful actions or betrayal and feeling wronged or "done to."
- Feeling of not being valued or worthwhile in the eyes of the spouse who committed the deceitful actions.
- Feeling overwhelmed around how to move forward especially since the betraying spouse has created a "train-wreck" mess of problems.
- Wondering or even questioning how the betraying spouse could ever be trusted again.

Martyrdom/ Feeling An Overwhelming Sense That Life Is Unfair

The term martyr means to makes great sacrifices or to suffer much in circumstances. In this phase of tunnel of feelings, spouses who have been deceived often experience a sense of martyrdom as they consider the fact that they have done nothing wrong and yet are forced to deal with the wreckage of their partner's betraying behaviours. Many deceived spouses at this point focus on all the personal sacrifices they have made in order to make the marriage work. In some cases, betrayed partners might rationalize how they have tolerated the faults of their spouses but still did not act-out or be dishonourable in the marriage. At this moment in the cycle, deceived spouses experience a tremendous sense of injustice and that the situations they experience as a result of their partners' deceptions really are not fair.

In the example with Julia, she starts to remember all of the times she tolerated her husband being emotionally-unavailable while he supposedly "worked on the computer." She did not complain to him and instead made accommodations by spending more time doing homework with the children. Meanwhile, he was

I Didn't Mean For This To Happen

having an emotional affair on the internet with a woman from Singapore. Julia feels the complete injustice and lack of fairness around how she was being the best parent for her children while her husband behaving immaturely as well as dishonourably by seeking the comfort from another woman outside of the marriage.

The Experience Of Being A Martyr:
- Remembering all the sacrifices you have made to make the marriage work which your deceiving spouse likely did not appreciate because they were too busy lying or engaging in dishonourable actions.
- Focusing on your own suffering and the complete injustice of the deceptions.
- Feeling like your deceiving spouse is immature, reckless, and insensitive.
- Wondering if your deceiving spouse is mentally-ill, sick, or devoid of morals.
- Focusing on your deceiving spouses shortcomings and character defects.
- Wondering why you did not see how wretched your deceiving partner could be before it was too late? Asking yourself if he/she was always this way (dishonourable) during your entire relationship?
- Wondering if your deceiving spouses' friends and family are aware of his/her faults and shortcomings?
- Remembering signs that there was something wrong with your deceiving spouse and that he/she had the potential to behave so badly.

Anger/Depression

Spouses who are deceived are likely to spend a lot of time reflecting on the unjust quality of their situations. Once they experience martyrdom as they remember all the good that they have done to make the marriage work while their partners were lying and acting deceptive, anger as well as rage is a common reaction. Anger is often the strong reaction to being wronged. In situations whereby there has been lying, manipulation, or even deception anger is a completely normal reaction.

When outwardly expressed, anger can communicated through strongly describing the injustice of being deceived. Such communication may be through a heightened inflection in voice that can sometimes become yelling or screaming. Some people demonstrate anger or rage by name-calling, threatening to hurt others, or even breaking objects. Many deceived spouses feel anger because they thought their partners were working towards the good of the marriage when in fact they were lying, being manipulative, or acting dishonourably. Sometimes deceived spouses break through a sense of being overwhelmed by the shock of the deception by finding their voices and expressing their feelings which comes through as anger.

In the example with Julia, she becomes furious once she processes fully the implications of her husband's emotional affair with a woman in Singapore. She is particularly upset around the injustice of this situation because now she has to contemplate whether she will uproot her entire family by filing for divorce because of her husband's reckless behaviour in a chat room on a computer. If she does not leave her husband, she feels like she now will have to go to couple's counselling sessions and waste time dealing with an issue that she never created in the first place. Now she is left with a legacy of hurt and has to deal with the emotional fall- out and wreckage from her husband's stupid decisions to cross marital boundaries by being seductive with that woman on the other side of the world.

I Didn't Mean For This To Happen

People can feel angry without outwardly expressing this emotion. Many professionals in the field of Psychology believe that when individuals feel like their angry outbursts will not be recognized, then they turn this anger inwards which can manifest into depression. Some individuals do not see the point of becoming angry because they feel hopeless to change their situations so what they do is begin emotionally shutting-down and withdrawing from life by struggling to get out of bed. This anger then is expressed as a disinterest with daily activities as individuals cope with problems more by sleeping or isolating from others. While feeling depressed, some individuals lose their appetite and find it difficult to attend to details or responsibilities. In situations whereby there has been deceit or even betrayal, some partners blame themselves for their spouses' dishonest actions by thinking they should have been better people or dealt with previous situations differently so that their loved ones were not deceitful. Such deceived partners collapse into a depression rather than deal with their problems of feeling overwhelmed by the pain of their marital issues of broken trust. Then there are others who become depressed but eat to give themselves emotional comfort so they end up eating in unhealthy ways without ever dealing with the underlying feelings of upset that they experience from the deception or betrayal.

Another way that anger can be expressed is in a passive-aggressive manner. This means that the deceived partner continues on in the marriage without resolving any of the difficulties around the dishonesty. The problem is that these spouses who have endured deceit are left over with their feelings of anger so they act-out these emotions by being emotionally difficult about other situations besides the deception. Such deceived spouses may nag or be critical of their partners without ever resolving the real issues around the betrayal that is occurring in the marriage. For example, Sally is upset about Marvin's compulsive spending habits with money. Sally does not communicate about this issue with Marvin because she knows he will become irritated as well as angry. Inside Sally is angry since Marvin spent all the money from their savings account on electronic gadgets. Rather than confronting Marvin, Sally becomes passive-aggressive and criticizes his driving, cooking, and other endeavours. She is irritable most of the time but she does not talk about the real issues that are bothering her deep down inside.

One final benefit of anger is that deceived spouses can feel powerful in their expression of their hostile feelings especially if their partners apologize or work hard to try to correct the past dishonourable transgressions. Many deceived spouses identify with anger because they do not want to feel vulnerable again. Perhaps the greatest fear for most spouses who have been deceived or betrayed is that if they let their guards down and learn to trust their spouses then they could end up in heartache if the dishonourable behaviour occurs again. There is one issue of going through this cycle of feelings the first time not knowing the amount of pain that is felt, but there is another major problem to go through these emotions again by suffering once more. On a figurative level, one cut from the deceit is painful but receiving a second cut with the compounded pain from the first cut in mind is immeasurable torture. Therefore staying angry is often a defense from fear of being hurt again in the future.

Now once deceived spouses have completed a full rotation through many of these feelings, they are likely to repeat through these same feelings except that they will move more quickly through the vulnerable and powerless phases. The emotional upset still churns with most deceived spouses now spending more time in the victim, martyr, and anger/depression phases. Some

I Didn't Mean For This To Happen

partners who have been betrayed will move through these phases simply by repeating the same questions in their minds which include: How could he/she do this to me and our family?, Doesn't he/she realize all the sacrifices that I made for this relationship?, and Does he/she realize how unfair this really is and the gigantic mess that they have created for us? As deceived spouses continue through these phases in the emotional pain, they may even become more enraged as they have visuals in their minds around the dishonourable behaviour. For example, Georga cannot stop thinking about her husband sitting in the chair drunk and unresponsive not caring about her needs, John remembers the moment he received the intercepted e-mail that revealed his wife's betrayal, Nora remembers the pain in her stomach as she opened the bill with the attached cheque that stated non-sufficient funds because her husband had spent all of their money, Marge can clearly see the moment in time in her mind when she caught her husband in his lie and so on.

Hurt/Emotional Abandonment

Deceived spouses (hurting parties) may or may not have to work through strong feelings of anger. If we look at feelings as a pyramid then shock as well as anger are at the tip of the pyramid. Underneath anger is a profound sense of hurt as well as emotional wounding that hurting parties feel because their spouses have gone outside of the marriage to meet emotional and/or sexual needs. Hurting parties may ask themselves: "Why wasn't I enough?" or "What was wrong with me that my partner had to do that?" When there is an identifiable person (mistress/lover) to which the acting-out party has gone to then that sense of hurt, emotional abandonment, as well as betrayal stings that much more because hurting parties often feel like they were somehow inadequate so this is why their partners acted-out with those people. As a result, hurting parties often feel emotional abandonment as if their partners have "tossed them under the bus" by disregarding their needs and going to an outside source (pornography, alcohol, sexual acting-out, spending of money, and so on) for comfort.

The feelings that we experience from broken trust come in waves and the challenge is to move through these emotions like travelling through a tunnel. There is a much brighter light on the other side. We have the opportunity to move through the lies and secrecy of the "acting-out behaviours" and the broken trust into the light of healing before God. There is nothing easy about moving through these feelings, but as we feel our emotions and move to a position of acceptance, we can then take the learning and grow on deeper emotional as well as spiritual levels. God does not waste a crisis and we can become stronger as well as better people for going through this adversity in our lives.

Chapter 2
How Did We Get Here?

Alyson dragged the large pile of laundry on to the top of the washing machine as a small slip of paper fell out of her husband's pants. She unfolded the delicate paper and found that it was a receipt for a withdrawal of fifteen thousand dollars. Alyson was confused and wrought with emotion as she scrambled to remember if there were any large purchases in her family recently? Perhaps they were the victim of identity theft? Alyson then checked the on-line banking records only to find that her husband had over-extended all of their credit cards to make advance cash withdrawals. Upon confronting her husband she quickly learned that he was trying to pay off a gambling debt. Alyson was sick to her stomach with fear and panic as she wondered- what just happened and how did we get to this point?

Many spouses of broken trust ask this same question as they query how they could have ended up in such situations whereby the futures of their relationships are called into question because of deceptions in their marriages. Rarely do individuals who lie or deceive wake up and decide that they will cause chaos, drama, as well as heartache in their marital relationships. Instead, the emotional upset that comes from broken trust behaviours is the end result of an insidious process whereby individuals who do the lying, cheating, or engaging in other dishonourable actions have begun to be dishonest with themselves long before they have acted out in their marriages. The reason why people break trust in marriages is unequivocally related to what I refer to as the golden trail of delusion whereby people lie to themselves first before they are enticed to act without integrity in their relationships.

The Golden Trail Of Delusion

When people decide to lie as well as act-out, they enter into an agreement with themselves whereby they are deciding to "**play in the shadows of life**." The shadows are filled with temptations, sins, and all kinds of behaviours that serve as distractions from other emotional issues. People mistake the danger of these self-destructive choices as excitement. For example, Ted is overwhelmed with his life and longs for the days when he had no responsibilities. He enters the *shadows of life* through lusting as he sexualizes women he sees before him. In Ted's mind this is his private world and his place where he can be free without responsibility while experiencing the rush of sexual arousal as endorphins, dopamine, as well as adrenaline pump through his brain. While aroused and in this fantasy-state, he is able to escape from his deeper feelings of restlessness as well as unhappiness in real life. As he masturbates he is triggering surges of dopamine which are "feel good brain chemicals." He thinks he is just a sexual guy, but in reality he is addicted to the surge of dopamine he is creating in himself through lusting and when the dopamine levels plummet he craves more so he continues on the path of sexually acting-out and lusting. Ted deludes himself that his "fantasies" are not harming anyone because after all he is not "touching" people. As he gets lost in these fantasies, Ted likes to take risks and sees the excitement factor in not just having these fantasies but also playing them out a bit with his flirting and "familiarity" with women particularly when his wife is not looking.

I Didn't Mean For This To Happen

Dishonourable actions in marriages such as lying, cheating, having affairs, abusing substances, gambling, being emotionally-unavailable, fantasy obsession, engaging in cybersex, and so on are all behaviours that are not events but are part of larger processes. Heartache and broken trust in relationships is a by-product of a bunch of actions usually over a range of time. Rarely do individuals purposely create broken trust and instead they are engaged in behaviours which they often see as solutions to their problems. The difficulty, however, is that these actions compound with the result being broken trust.

One of the most confusing statements people who break trust in relationships say to their spouses and families is: "I never meant to hurt you!" In response, many heartbroken spouses often reply: "Well, what were you thinking when you did that?" The problem is that individuals who lie and/or act deceptive in their marriages are not thinking and are instead putting in place a chain of events based on their own microscopic perceptions of what are the right courses of action in those early moments before trust was broken in their marriages. In essence, people who end up deceiving others often lie to themselves first before they end up hurting the people they care most about in life.

Entering The Shadows

This process of lying to ourselves is really about self-delusion which means that people convince themselves that reality is a certain way and they act out of those misperceptions. In the beginning, acting-out parties will often tell themselves unhelpful stories such as they are not understood by others, that they sacrifice so much with little appreciation from the people around them, they are missing out on life because of all of their responsibilities and so on. In essence, these individuals develop narrow, tunnel vision as they focus on small details in life and exaggerate their reactions immensely which results in a loss of full or proper perspective. A person may be stressed at a moment in life, however, with self-delusion they convince themselves that the "sky is falling" and that they are forced to deal with circumstances that are somehow unfair on a personal level.

Many people who end up breaking trust will "awfulize" situations in their lives by believing that they are overwhelmed, life is difficult, nobody cares about them, and so on. Other individuals in these same situations may even believe that others need them and they are responsible for everyone else's issues. In all of the variations of these situations, individuals who are prone to acting dishonourably in their relationships begin with telling themselves unhelpful ideas around who they are in relation to others and then they work themselves into a driven, negative, stressed, anxious, angry, or fearful state. Such individuals have started the trip down the golden path of delusion. People may feel stress, but they will inflame these pressures as an excuse to *play in the shadows of life* with their acting-out behaviours.

These same acting-out parties continue to obsess about how over-worked, over-burdened, stressed, or needed they are in their lives. Usually in these delusions, individuals focus on their self-sacrifices and give themselves honourable intentions. People may have feelings of being a victim or taken advantage of by others around them. Then some individuals martyr themselves as they focus on the ways they help others without being appreciated. Suddenly, a disguised opportunity (the acting-out behaviours or the *shadows of life*) comes along and these same people who are drowning in responsibilities, crippled by depression, feeling underappreciated and so on believe they can now *seek the relief they think they deserve*. The momentum is in place as they continue to walk further down the golden trail of delusion.

I Didn't Mean For This To Happen

For example, Ben is a hard-working family man who spends long hours working and has the responsibility of being the breadwinner for his wife as well as four children. He believes he gives all the time so he is overwhelmed, and now it is time for him to "give to himself" as he engages in watching pornographic images on-line. Ben has started the process of *playing in the shadows of life* by looking at pornography. He knows his wife would not approve but in his self-deluded thinking he lies to himself as he remembers all the sacrifices he has made of working so hard and earning all this money. He feels old and burdened with responsibility so now it is his time to "have some fun" because after all he rarely is able to go out with his friends on Friday nights like he did in his younger days. Ben is lying to himself and he is firmly planted on the golden trail of delusion as he justifies being able to spend even more time watching pornography apart from his family. Furthermore, Ben's self-delusions are very helpful because he can use these falsehoods of how he is so overburdened to not take responsibility for his life and now he has a free pass to engage in the acting-out behaviours of his choice. He has justified himself into a position of being able to watch pornography with very little guilt.

Shane loves to flirt and play with Nancy the Youth Director at the Church. She "brings out the young side" of his character. Nancy is an opportunity of escape for Shane because he can forget about the job he despises and can ignore the repetitive, nagging demands of his wife. Shane starts to *play in the shadows of life*. In fact, Shane tells himself that his wife's idea of a good time is to hand him a list of chores and then scold him when he has not completed certain tasks on time. Shane "awfulizes" his marriage by telling himself that he ended up marrying a woman that was like his own Mother. The reality is that Shane has started the descent down the golden trail of delusion as he crosses more boundaries by spending time with Nancy and making sexual overtures outside of his marriage. Shane is actively *playing in the shadows of life* with his lusting as well as sexual advances towards Nancy.

How We Become Lost In The Shadows

Once people begin to *play in the shadows of life*, they will venture further along the golden trail of delusion as they start to cross the limits that they may have set for themselves. For example, Alysons's husband starts "chasing losses" (spending additional money on gambling in an attempt to make up for the money he has lost) as he gets further into more gambling debt, Ben spends longer amounts of time viewing pornography, and Shane is now fantasizing about having a sexual relationship with Nancy. Charles is not adulterous, addicted to substances, or even interested in pornography but he is obsessed with work. He is expanding his company internationally and gives up opportunities to come home to visit his family because he is obsessed with building his empire. Therefore Charles is starting to break trust in his marriage because he is consumed by his work and has no time for his family. Charles is *playing in the shadows of life* because he is driven by his ego for success even though he has convinced himself that it is God's will that he expand his company across the world at the expense of his family relationships. In reality, Charles is driven by *impact ego* (the desire to make a difference and create impact which is motivated by self-glory) by making his company even larger as well as more profitable.

At some point Alyson's husband the problem gambler, Ben with the porn fantasy obsession, Shane the potential adulterer, and Charles the workaholic should realize that their behaviours are becoming problematic before their actions reach a crisis point in their marriages right? The problem is that when they begin to experience shame or guilt, they initially feel a rush of excitement related to their actions. When Alyson's husband maxes his credit card to pay off a gambling debt he feels guilty, but he is also excited as he wonders if this final amount of money he can get from a cash advance will be his big win to pay off all the other debts? He teeters on the verge of self-destruction but instead of coming to his senses around how incredibly ridiculous he is acting by spending all of his family's money, he is focused on the danger as well as thrill of his behaviours. He wonders if he can break out of his debt cycle with one roll of the dice in his gambling adventures? The intensity becomes a fog that settles over to conceal any rational judgement.

Likewise, Ben knows his family is sitting in the next room and that his four year old daughter may walk into his den at any moment to see that he is masturbating to pornographic images. Rather than coming to his senses and feeling guilty for his actions, the thrill of his wife walking in and catching him being bad clouds his judgement. On a logical level, Ben understands that he could traumatize his child and wife and if they ever saw him naked viewing pornography and that his wife may even divorce him, however, he gambles that he will not get caught in these dishonourable actions. There is an intensity that comes with the feeling of potentially being caught and Ben is so microscopically focused on the rush of his self-destructive behaviours that he continues to watch even more pornography. Ben loves his family, however, he is mood-altering himself and fuelling the excitement as well as adrenaline rush of viewing extra pornographic images with the risk of getting caught.

Shane loves his wife, even though at that moment he is convinced that she is a nag. When he flirts with Nancy he is on a sexual conquest. If he can hold Nancy's hand he is filled with excitement. He touches the bottom of her skirt with the brush of his finger tips and he feels a charge of emotional as well as sexual electricity. With this intensity of his actions, he is able to escape from the self-delusional pain he feels from the responsibility of being married. He believes his soul yearns to be single and carefree even though he is a proud family man.

Charles knows his marriage with his wife could disintegrate if he stays out of the country for even longer periods of time. On a logical level, he understands that his relationships with his young children are suffering because he is away so much with work on an international scale. He escapes from all these worries by focusing on the intense rush of expanding his company or empire. Charles convinces himself that he is making these sacrifices for his family so they can have a good life, but the reality is that Charles is already wealthy. He does not consider the line between earning money and destroying family relationships because he is obsessed with work so the result is that he is emotionally unavailable to his loved ones.

In all of these situations there are red flags or warnings that these individuals above are spiralling out of control. For example Alyson's husband is spending money on gambling that he does not have, Ben is viewing pornography on a computer accessed by his children and while they are home, Shane is married and is flirting with another woman, and Charles rarely sees his family because he is working most months out of the country. Individuals who play in the shadows of life and end up breaking trust in their relationships do not stop to focus on the entire ramifications of their behaviours. Instead, they perceive the intensity they are experiencing as a sign that they should plunge further into their self-destructive behaviours. As a result, these people are not only

I Didn't Mean For This To Happen

walking down the golden trail of delusion, but they are doing so with blinders over their eyes.

Emotional Blinders

Just like the horse with the carriage wears blinders so that he is not scared by oncoming traffic, so do people wear a type of emotional blinder that keeps them from recognizing the consequences of their decisions. This way they can keep on behaving in dishonourable ways experiencing the rush of intensity, without coming to terms with the ramifications of their behaviours. These emotional blinders are types of thinking traps that are referred to as various names throughout the field of Psychology. With these thinking traps, people never personally challenge their own falsehoods or self-delusional thinking and instead they can keep doing what they are doing without ever changing their actions. Some thinking traps include *minimization* (minimizing the consequences of actions), *rationalization* (justifying poor decisions or behaviours), *projection* (blaming others for issues while disregarding personal responsibility), and *denial* (not accepting that there is even a problem.)

When people ***play with the shadows of life***, they have found an escape place in their minds whereby they can hide from deeper emotional issues and from themselves. With a focus of distraction, they can immerse themselves into the pornography, lusting, fantasy obsessions, on-line gaming, gambling, compulsive spending and so on. Such people begin to **compartmentalize** as they believe that one area of life does not impact the other. In fact, some people even believe that what others do not know will not hurt them. These individuals who start acting-out with self-destructive behaviours are merrily skipping down the *golden trail of delusion* and the emotional train is in motion as there will be a collision of impact between the secret world they are building for themselves and real life.

How We Play In The Shadows Of Life

Therefore lies and deceit (pretending to do something while doing something else) are the ingredients that pave the way for broken trust. There is a freedom in marriages for people to come and go as they please and this liberty includes mutual spouses' beliefs that when they are not together that they are each acting with honour as well as integrity. Of course there are numerous ways that people can deceive each other and the following is a skeletal outline of different types of acting-out behaviours as people *play in the shadows of life*.

Playing In The Shadows Of Life With Lies

The most common way that trust is broken in relationships is through lies. People will use lies as a way to deceive others into believing that they are being good as well as honourable, but really they are engaging in the opposite types of behaviours that are not virtuous. Lying is also a technique that individuals can use to "buy a type of insurance" which means that they can keep doing what they want such as spending money frivolously, engaging in affairs, abusing drugs or alcohol, and so on and if they are caught then they can use lies like insurance to get out of the consequences associated with their behaviours. For example, with car insurance a person can drive in a reckless manner and if they crash their car, the insurance they have will cover most of the expenses associated with the damage to their vehicle which means they do not have to suffer from the entire financial consequences of driving in such a destructive manner. Likewise, individuals can be emotionally reckless in their relationships by acting in a dishonourable way such as spending excess money, crossing personal boundaries by flirting or sexually seducing others outside of the marriage, fuel-

I Didn't Mean For This To Happen

ling their fantasy obsessions with pornography, and so on. If their spouses catch them in these behaviours, they use lies by denying what they are doing as a type of insurance so that they do not get into trouble. As with the game of Monopoly, lies can serve as the "get out of jail card for free" pass in life so that people can do what they want without ever having to be accountable for their actions.

On many levels, people can use lying as a vehicle to satisfy their needs for instant gratification. A common saying is "It is easier to beg for forgiveness later than it is to ask for permission in the first place." This means that individuals can do whatever it is they want and minimize the consequences of such actions either through lying, spinning the truth, or asking for forgiveness later. For example, Larry may really want to go out with his friends Friday night but he knows if he asks his wife Tracy that she will be upset because she is wanting to spend some couple's time together and he has already been out with his friends three times already that week. Rather than come home and deal with her anger, Larry stays late at work and leaves a message on Tracy's cell phone knowing that she is on route home and will not pick up her cell phone while she is driving. Larry says he will be late at work and that Tracy should not wait up for him. He knows she will be furious, but he really wants to hang out with his guy friends that evening. His friend Jay just got a new car and he wants to see this vehicle. Larry gets what he wants (seeing his friends) and then either begs for forgiveness yet again or uses some type of lie to justify his disappearance. Thus, such people can satisfy their selfish needs in the moment without worrying about ramifications, except that of course, trust is often broken in the process.

Types of Lies

The technique of lying crosses an entire continuum all the way from "white lies" or what could be referred to as "spinning" the truth to pathological lying whereby individuals lie constantly out of habit and with no associated benefit. The following includes the gamut of lies people can create.

Omission of Details

Many people convince themselves that they are not lying because they are telling the truth. The problem is that they omit significant details and do not offer up important information that would allow other people to see a fuller perspective of what is going on in situations. Individuals with this pattern are elusive and often believe that knowledge is power so they do not want other people to have influence over them so as a result they do not open up about a lot of details particularly related to having to be accountable.

An example:

Joe leaves his wife for the evening to go and visit another couple's house. This other couple named Tina and Gordon live down the street. Upon arriving home from the visit Joe's wife asks him how he enjoyed the visit? He replies by saying he had a good visit at their home, but fails to mention that Gordon was out of town on business and that he was meeting with Tina specifically because she was complaining about problems in her marriage with Gordon. Tina described how Gordon works all of the time and rarely has time for her as well as their children.

Omitted Detail #1: Yes, Joe was visiting Tina and Gordon's house but Gordon was not home.

Omitted Detail #2: Tina was confiding in Joe about her marital problems.

Omitted Detail #3: Tina confessed to Joe that she was attracted to him and that she wished she had an understanding relationship like Joe had with his wife.

I Didn't Mean For This To Happen

Omitted Detail #4: Tina and Gordon's children were not home at this house so Tina as well as Joe were alone together.

Omitted Detail #5: Tina started crying about the loneliness that she felt in her marriage with Gordon. Joe reached over to give her a comforting hug.

Omitted Detail #6: Tina accepted this hug as affection and kissed Joe. Now Joe has returned home pretending that nothing different has happened other than a regular visit to Tina and Gordon's house. Joe convinces himself he has not lied because technically his wife did not ask him if he had kissed Tina. If she had asked, then he says to himself that of course he would have told her the truth. Joe suppresses any guilt feelings by convincing himself he was truthful because he did attend that location and the kiss was an accident after all. Why would he purposely hurt his wife by telling her about a kiss that meant nothing with Tina right?

Through an omission of all of these details, Joe has been deceptive and has distorted the truth by not offering more information. Instead, he presents this situation as a regular visit that he would have made any day of the week without declaring critical information such as the fact that he was alone with another man's wife and committed adultery.

White Lies or Spinning The Truth

With this type of lie, a person stretches a version of the truth in order to give themselves honourable intentions. There is a thread of truth in the described situation, but the details are exaggerated in the lying person's descriptions of events.

An Example:

Sam and Leslie have a joint account whereby if they are short on any expenses, they can go to this bank account to cover the costs. Usually this money is set aside for unexpected bills that need to be covered for the children's sports activities or medical expenses and so on. Leslie discovered that this account which holds thousands of dollars has been completely drained the day before. She is wanting to make a payment for their oldest son's orthodontic work and he also has a hockey camp coming up in the next month so she wanted to purchase new goalie pads for him. At first, she believes that she is the victim of identity theft because her husband never mentioned spending any money and their agreement was that they would openly communicate and keep each other up to date about the funds in the account. Upon further investigation, Leslie discovers that Sam has spent the remaining funds on a new large screen television with a surround sound system equipped with the latest in technological applications. When Leslie confronts Sam about his expenditures, he admits that he purchased all of these electronics as a gift for the family. In particular, he would like to invite his friends over to watch mixed martial arts challenges on pay per view but he thought the family could benefit as well.

Sam has "spun the truth" because his real intention was to be selfish and purchase all of this electronic equipment as a way to impress his friends during their social gatherings. In this case, Sam assigns himself honourable intentions by pretending that he is considering the family's needs when really he just wants new technological gadgets. Essentially, he has chosen his own selfish indulgence over his son's orthodontic and sports needs. Sam has violated the agreement by using this account for his own personal interests and he has betrayed the trust in the relationship by not joining with Leslie as a team for the larger welfare of their children. Instead, they are now working at cross purposes because he is more focused on his needs.

Exaggerations

Some people have fears that they are not good enough as they are so they concentrate their energies on creating an image

I Didn't Mean For This To Happen

or a persona for themselves. They pretend that they are confident and that they "have it all together". One vehicle for inflating self-image is to embellish stories or "stretch the truth." A common example would be "fishing stories" whereby people talk about the big fish they caught that got away and the drama that ensued. In reality, there was no fish or the fish that was caught was slightly larger than a minnow but the story sounds good and people end up looking like exceptional fishermen.

One difficulty with exaggerations is that individuals can lose themselves through the process of creating large personas filled with all kinds of exaggerations. Such people are so focused on being better than everyone else, looking important, or playing the role of a "big shot" that they often glare at others with ridicule as they try to position themselves as "top of the pack" or as super competent with no personal flaws whatsoever. These people who constantly exaggerate lose a sense of genuineness or authenticity in their relationships with others because they are so preoccupied with trying to "look good." Similarly, trust can be broken in relationships because individuals are so focused on building up lies or exaggerations and appearing confident that they do so in all areas of their lives. The partners of people who constantly exaggerate never have a sense of calm in their relationships because they do not trust the truth of what their lying spouses are saying at any given moment in time or they are worried about when all of these stories and exaggerations will be discovered by others. Such spouses of people who exaggerate often live in fear of impending embarrassment as they worry about others seeing through the stories and detecting the lies.

An Example:

Henry was a very prideful man and quite the story-teller. Tia was initially attracted to his charm and his outgoing personality when they first started dating and eventually they were married. Together Henry and Tia were a very social couple and regularly invited people over from the church. Henry loved to show off his technology and would brag about the large prices he had paid for these material items. Tia loved to be around other people, but she always felt queasy in her stomach as she worried if Henry's exaggerations were noticeable to others. She vowed to herself that she would not try and embarrass him so she was always silent during his story-telling moments. Henry was showing Garry the latest addition to his technological collection which included special wave surround sound speakers. Henry boasted that these speakers had been specifically imported from an on-line store in Europe. Garry appeared confused as he said: "Henry, I think you got ripped off here because those same speakers are at our local furniture store here in town and I have read the reviews and they aren't all that great!" Tia leaned against the wall to steady herself as she felt a wave of anxiety churning in her stomach.

Story-Telling and Balancing Lies

Another form of lying is when individuals tell people a number of different lies and then they try and balance these stories. Over time, people who lie can forget who they told what detail to and then their story of what happened continues to change. The result is that the lying spouse may engage others in a type of "cat and mouse game" whereby the partner is trying to seek out the truth by investigating or even "catching them in a lie." For example, the receiver of the lies tries to confront the lying person about the various versions of the truth. When this occurs, the lying individual just keeps creating more stories and the truth rarely does surface.

The lying and story-telling serves as a distraction because people who lie can keep others confused. Individuals who are be-

I Didn't Mean For This To Happen

ing lied to may spend an inordinate time trying to figure the facts from the fiction. Meanwhile, the person who is doing all of the lying is off indulging in their dishonourable behaviours. Such lies serve as a smokescreen of protection that keeps others at an emotional distance because those people are consumed in trying to sort out the truth.

An Example:

Chris is the head musician at the church and he coordinates the music program for services. Abigail is his wife and together they have a young daughter who is three months old. Since the birth, Abigail has been suffering from a bit of post-partum blues but she does not want to appear to be an ungrateful mother so she confides in no one about her struggles. Lately, Chris has been missing his rehearsal meetings at the church. He tells Abigail that he is fine and that he has been regularly attending these meetings. Meanwhile, all kinds of Church Elders have been calling the house wondering where Chris is and the whereabouts of his location. When confronted, Chris changes his story regularly by telling his wife and the other people that he has had car problems, he has a chronic back injury that he is struggling with, Abigail is crashing into a depression and he is helping her with the baby, as well as all kinds of other excuses. People want to extend emotional support to Chris so they give Abigail the opportunity of counselling sessions, offer to help to fix the family van that is not broken, and share compassion for Chris' back as well as broken collarbone for when he fell off of the ladder. Over time, Chris' excuses keep changing and no one knows the truth. The reality is that Chris is feeling overwhelmed as a new parent and with life in general. He is depending more on isolating with alcohol as a way to cope. He keeps everyone around him confused as they try to sort through his pile of excuses and lies. Meanwhile, he stays isolated drinking himself into an oblivion of alcohol.

Denial and Blame

Some people lie as a way to protect themselves from the shame and guilt of their behaviours. Also, such individuals can buy more time as well as space if they blame others for their problems rather than taking personal responsibility for their actions. One way that people protect themselves from being accountable for behaviours is through denial. These individuals deny there is a problem or that they have done anything wrong.

This type of denial may be in the form of a bold face lie in which the person outright denies the truth of what is going on in a situation or this same individual may admit what they are doing but blame others as they justify their actions.

An Example of Denial:

Barry has a fantasy obsession with pornography. He tells himself that he just needs to relax from the stress of work and since he is a guy with a high sex drive, this is one way for him to unwind after a long day. He habitually views pornographic images on his home computer. Jillian is on a website looking up dinner recipes when an instant pop-up message from a pornographic website offers a gateway connection to another porn site. In the moment, Jillian is confused and deletes the pop-up message. Then she wonders why the message would be addressed to her husband's e-mail address? She confronts him with this information. Barry says that the computer probes must have gotten his e-mail while he was surfing the internet. He denies ever being on a pornography website and vows that he will get better firewall software so that such probes no longer access their personal information. Essentially, Barry is denying the problem of his fantasy obsession and uses a false intention of buying better computer security when

I Didn't Mean For This To Happen

he has no plans to change his behaviours. He uses his promise of purchasing such protective software for the computer as a way of buying time and keeping Jillian at a distance as she believes this situation is resolved when, in reality, Barry is sinking further into what is now becoming a stronger obsession with pornography.

An Example of Blame:

Let's take the above example with Jillian and Barry to a further extreme. After Barry promises to buy protective computer software, Jillian finds a file stored in Barry's computer documents. In the virtual file folder, there are countless numbers of pornographic images which Barry has obviously saved off of the internet. Jillian confronts Barry about this stored file. Barry admits that he has been viewing pornographic images, but he justifies these actions as he blames Jillian for being sexually-repressed or frigid. He retorts: "Jillian if you didn't deny me my sexual needs then I wouldn't have to get pleasure from a machine. You knew when you married me that I was a man with a large need for sex. For years you have been rejecting me and what else am I supposed to do? I am a loyal man and have taken our Christian marital vows very seriously so in order to remain faithful to you, I have to have an outlet of some kind!" Jillian feels guilty that she has not been sexually-available for Barry and vows that she will be more understanding of his needs.

Meanwhile, Barry has bought more time as well as space through his manipulation of blaming Jillian. He justifies his fantasy obsession with pornography and now Jillian leaves him alone as she second-guesses her own worth in this relationship. She is convinced that she is the one with the problem. She initiates sex with Barry, however, he does not reciprocate because he tells her that she has been so sexually-disinterested in their relationship for such a long time that he has just resolved himself to satisfying his own sexual needs. Jillian feels like she has been a failure in this marriage and obsesses about what she has done wrong. Unfortunately, Barry's marital problems continue to progress because his obsession with pornography just intensifies as he becomes desensitized to the images on the computer screen. In order to be sexually-aroused he needs even more violent forms of pornography in order to peek his interest. The trust between Jillian and her husband continues to erode because he still lies about his need for these sexual images, and Jillian just resolves herself to the fact that there is something wrong with her. This is such an embarrassing issue that neither spouse reaches out for help and they both continue a façade that they are a happy Christian couple who have absolute love and devotion for each other. Outside people in the church community are even envious of their relationship without knowing the real details of what is happening within their marriage.

Barry and Jillian can remain stuck in this emotional holding pattern for a long time because he uses blame as a way to justify his fantasy obsession with pornography. In this case, Barry never takes responsibility for his lack of communication or his refusal to work on repairing the marriage. Instead, Barry assigns blame to Jillian which she accepts out of her own insecurities and they do not progress as a couple because of their reluctance to get help for their situation.

False Promises

With this form of lying, people try to convince themselves that they have intentions which they do not really want to act upon. When caught with bad behaviours, such individuals say they want to change and promise to take positive action to resolve problems but their promises are false because they really have no motivation to positively transform their situations. Thus,

I Didn't Mean For This To Happen

these types of people buy time or emotional space from others by pretending to go along with a solution. In fact, they *want to want to change* but are not really motivated to do the work necessary to create sustainable differences in their lives.

An Example:

Let's return to the example of Chris and Abigail. Remember that she is the mother of a three month old baby and her husband is the Head Musician of the music program at the church. Chris creates all kinds of lies in order to cover up the reality that he is drinking alcohol in order to solve his problems.

When Abigail confronts him about his drinking, he admits that he has been drinking too much lately and that his consumption of alcohol has impacted his abilities to not only be a good husband and father, but he has also failed in keeping up his responsibilities as Head Musician at the Church. He thanks Abigail for bringing this problem to his attention and vows that he will resolve his drinking issues immediately. Abigail walks away from the conversation feeling better knowing that now she and Chris can openly communicate about his drinking problems.

The difficulty, however, is that in this example Chris has no motivation to change. He is attached to drinking alcohol as a way to seek relief from stress in his life. For Chris the thought of giving up alcohol is overwhelming and he does not think that he can manage situations properly. Chris convinces himself that he has an issue with anxiety in his life and alcohol helps him balance out his emotions properly. Chris *wants to want to* stop drinking, but he also is not ready to give up the relief that he thinks alcohol provides for him. He agrees with Abigail as a way of getting her to stop nagging him about his drinking issue. Meanwhile, he continues to quietly isolate with drink in hand. Now he is just going to be more creative so that people do not detect that drinking is an issue in his life. Chris believes that if he masks the smell of alcohol, then he can just show up to the music rehearsals numb with alcohol but not overtly drunk and no one will notice. This way he can stop getting into trouble for not taking his music responsibility seriously and he can still seek relief in alcohol.

Habitual and Pathological Lying

Some people are focused on having the freedom to do whatever it is that they want in life without having to be responsible or accountable to anyone. If they are caught doing bad behaviours, then they just lie as a way of looking like they have honourable intentions but in reality they still are able to do whatever it is that they want to at the time. Therefore lying becomes a type of habit and a means for getting out of trouble. Over time, some people lie so much that this becomes their primary way of coping in life and they forget when they are lying. Such lying behaviour comes so naturally for these people that lying is an automatic response.

In these instances, such chronic liars will lie just for the sake of lying and they do not have a hidden motive or objective. Instead, these people just want to keep people confused and at an emotional distance. Chronic liars do not want to release information about themselves because they believe such details can be used against them at a later time. Also these same people are careful to divide parts of their lives into sections so that they have friends who do not know or have contact with each other and there are numerous social circles that these people keep separate. In fact, chronic liars never want too many people who know them to be in the same room together because in such social situations these outside individuals may compare the liar's previous stories or lies. Therefore in these instances chronic liars may have their covers blown when people are able to communicate with each other to sort through details or stories they have been told in the past.

I Didn't Mean For This To Happen

Some chronic liars operate at a pathological level and want to create such strong divisions amongst the people they know that they set these individuals up against each other so that they are busy fighting or arguing rather than bonding and sharing mutual stories. Chronic liars may position people against each other by gossiping and saying that one person said bad words about another person. Then these chronic liars say that this information is a secret and that no one should talk about this underlying animosity because there should not be any bad feelings being shared out in the open. As a result, these two people end up being caught up in a silent anger with each other without ever getting together to compare stories or detect that they are being set up by the chronic liar with whom they both have a friendship or association.

In this way, chronic liars can create instant chaos as people end up fighting or arguing with each other over perceived insults. Meanwhile, chronic liars are off participating further in their bad behaviours without detection because people are so busy arguing that they are never able to align and compare stories by realizing that their mutual lying friend is the source of all of the chaos. The result is what can be referred to as "crazy-making" whereby the recipients of the lies feel like they are going crazy trying to sort through the chaos and emotional upset while the chronic liar behaves as if there are no problems at all.

An Example:

Hank is what people would refer to as a "wheeler-dealer." He is always meeting people and making deals. In fact, Hank has a number of strengths as a salesman. The problem is that Hank has been taking money from people on bad investments. He says that he has inside information and lures individuals into investing. Gloria is Hank's wife and she is an active member in the church. Hank enthusiastically attends church events because he believes that this is a great networking opportunity and he can gain more investors. At this event, Gloria is going to let people know about some exciting plans to expand the Sunday School program room with new renovations which have come in through some recent donations. Hank feels a little threatened because some of his previous investors are at this same event and Gloria will undoubtedly draw people together as she shares her excitement about the new Sunday School renovations. At the event, Hank is anxious and he leans over to Gloria to mention that he heard some other members of the church talking about her and saying that she was a loudmouth who bragged all the time about her accomplishments. In fact, Hank says he heard others referring to her as "Gloria who thinks she's so great." Gloria's bubble of enthusiasm is burst and she is now self-consciously trying to detect who amongst the members of the group would say such vicious words? Meanwhile, Hank is free "to work the room" and he lines up a new potential investor in site well out of the way of the other people who have contributed into his other investment schemes. Hank has accomplished a divide as well as conquer maneuver so that Gloria does not unite the group with her discussions and the past investors do not even notice that Hank is in the room. Instead, Gloria is off in the corner of the room worrying about who is talking badly behind her back. Gloria does not even question Hank about using church events to sell investments because she is so upset by the supposed actions of the gossiping people.

Passive-Aggressive Lying

Some people are *resentful pleasers* in that they do what other people want them to do because they fear conflict. These individuals are so preoccupied with looking good or honourable that they do not want other people to think badly of them. Therefore, resentful pleasers will go along with what others want from them,

I Didn't Mean For This To Happen

but they will get even later because they feel controlled in such situations. For example, some wives will give their husbands lots of lists of chores that need to be done and then nag them if these tasks are not completed. Rather than communicating the fact that they feel controlled, over-burdened, or nagged such husbands will reluctantly accomplish these duties and feel resentful. One way of acting out this resentment is to set up the other spouse to look like a bad person. Therefore resentful pleasers are usually nice and mild-mannered because they always appear helpful as well as concerned about everyone else's needs. Thus when these pleasers are asked to do something by their spouses they may appear lazy or indifferent to such requests. As a result, spouses need to become loud and boisterous in order to get the attention of these resentful pleasers. In this dynamic, resentful pleasers appear to the outside world as nice people who are being controlled or "henpecked" (nagged) by their mean as well as unappreciative spouses. The hidden laziness demonstrated by resentful pleasers is actually an act of retaliation as they take back their own wills and accomplish tasks on their own time and according to their own control. Meanwhile, the outside world witnesses these resentful pleasers' hard work ethic because the apparent laziness is only witnessed in private by their partners.

When this pattern is continued onward, resentful pleasers delight in taking back their control so they purposefully try to make their "controlling" spouses angry and then make a public display of how they feel like they are not appreciated. Resentful pleasers may also make up lies as a passive-aggressive tactic to take back their own control in their relationships while appearing good as well as honourable to the outside world. Therefore spouses of resentful pleasers grow even more angry because they are trying to wade through these lies. To the outside world, such resentful pleasers appear to be victims of their mean, controlling, and nasty partners. The reality is that these resentful pleasers keep setting up their partners through their passive-aggressive actions of being lazy, refusing to be controlled, and taking back their control through lying. Some resentful pleasers even delight in being clever and that their spouses do not know about their lies. This way resentful pleasers can gain back some control on their own terms.

An Example:

Bart would regularly come home from work and metamorphosize into a slug on the couch by being emotionally-unavailable in his marriage. He was consumed with work stress and the last thing he felt like doing at the end of the day was talking since most of his work schedule involved intense sales meetings. He found the entire conversation around how he was doing and what was new with his work day to be nauseating so he made sure that he would disengage with his wife and just grunt in responses to her attempts to connect as well as bond. In return, Elaine (Bart's wife) would become furious and as a bid for control she would hand him a list of chores that he needed to do in order to maintain the household. Then she would criticize him for his lack of attentiveness to their marriage. Bart was a resentful pleaser so he would put on a fake smile, take his list, and work through the list of household chores. Elaine would query him around what he had done so far and then blame him for not taking the time to eat dinner with her.

Bart would regain control, however, during social events. In his resentful pleasing way, Bart offered to get Elaine the special appetizers for their next church function. They were in a hurry and Elaine had bragged about these amazing frozen appetizers she had recently located at the grocery store. She rushed out to the trunk of the car to grab the appetizers that Bart had promised to pro-

I Didn't Mean For This To Happen

vide. There was a large brown paper grocery bag filled with beets. Bart was socializing with the other elders of the Church when Elaine escorted Bart out of the room while trying to suppress her increasing rage. Elaine said: "Bart you promised you would get those new appetizers from the freezer isle and I have a trunk full of beets!" With a supportive gaze and clever grin, Bart responded: "Elaine dear I got you the appetizers and they must have fallen out of the bag." Then Bart glided into the room with an extra enthusiastic kick in his step. Elaine was miserable and criticized Bart as being an incompetent husband in her discussions with the other wives. Meanwhile, Bart poured a cup of coffee and delivered it by hand to Elaine as he reached over to plant a subtle kiss on her cheek. He said: "Here you go sweetheart! I know you haven't been feeling well lately." Elaine was seething in rage because she knew Bart had deliberately purchased a bag of beets and that he was being passive-aggressive as well as lying. The people in the room glared at Elaine as they wondered how this horrible lady could be so unappreciative and cold towards her loving husband?

The Emotional Cost of Lying

The problem with lying is that the people who create the deceit get to buy emotional space or time to engage in bad behaviours. This solution does not, however, come without a cost. In such situations individuals who lie accumulate emotional interest. They do not have to pay for consequences in the moment because they escape from trouble by lying, but eventually these lies do catch up with them.

An initial cost is that out of lying, an emotional divide is created in the relationship. A marital couple who is supposed to work together as a team towards a shared vision of their future or a higher purpose end up operating at cross-purposes. One spouse is trying to get away with behaviours and defend themselves while the other takes on the role of investigating or detecting the truth. The lying partner then uses blame as well as justification as a way to rationalize their behaviours, while the other person becomes more focused on tracking them down by determining "the truth" at all costs. A huge difficulty in this situation is that each side becomes invested in "being right" and justifying their positions. Furthermore, instead of loving each other, spouses relate to each other by being on the attack or defence as they prepare for another battle around the truth because lying as well as escaping from ever communicating properly is the primary mode or modus operandi for lying partners.

In such relationships where lying occurs trust is inevitably broken and loving couples emotionally separate themselves by becoming opposing team members. Situations are never resolved because each side is working against each other. The lying partner is either escaping through more story-telling or trying to recruit others into agreeing with them that they are justified in their actions. Meanwhile, spouses who are being lied to will often either isolate in the shame of their problems by keeping their issues a secret or even pretend to the outside world that everything fine. In some instances these spouses on the receiving end of the lies will attempt to recruit friends and family to support them in their dissatisfaction with their lying partners. In such situations, couples can become positioned into teams operating against each other.

Sometimes people lie as a cover for bad behaviours which can include emotional or even physical affairs with people outside of the marriage. Now let's examine how trust in marriages can become broken when partners act out through emotional or physical affairs with others which they may convince themselves are initially harmless.

Playing In The Shadows With Lusting

The behaviours which we will refer to as emotional affairs run along a continuum as well. Emotional affairs include actions

I Didn't Mean For This To Happen

whereby one partner is acting out in an inappropriate way with people outside of the marriage and these interactions have a seductive quality. At one end of the spectrum, this could include flirting which is playful behaviour intended to arouse sexual interest all the way to sexual discussions through chat rooms or telephone conversations to sexual acts on web cams through the internet whereby two people are *technically* not touching each other. With pre-affair behavior, people can experience an ego boost that someone else sees their *specialness* as they feel desired as well as admired in some way. These boosts to their ego can then become part of a thought cycle whereby people think about how desired they are in their fantasy minds which gets them excited.

Flirting

Many people believe that flirting is harmless and in some ways it can be an innocent action or part of a humorous exchange of words. For example, there is a social gathering of friends at a barbeque. Mona moves along the table and reaches over with her fork to try and get a slice of tomato. She accidentally brushes up against Tom and loses balance. Her fork touches his arm and during this clumsy moment Tom says: "Whoah, Mona keep that weapon to yourself" and he laughs. Tina (a mutual friend of the group) calls out: "Hey Tom I bet that's the most action you're going to see all night" and she winks at his wife Sally. Tom giggles and calls out: "Thanks Mona, you rocked my world baby!" Mona laughs and blushes knowing that her action with her fork was not a sexual overture. All of these people return to their corners with their friends and spouses as the evening progresses. Tom, Mona, Sally, and Tina just continue on with the barbeque and the interaction was harmless.

In the above example, flirting was a silly reaction to a clumsy as well as awkward social moment. There were sexual innuendos, but no seduction was involved. Seduction means to entice someone to stray from right behaviour. Now "right behaviour" is relative and can be interpreted in many different ways. Let's examine, however, the marital commitment of a Christian marriage. Spouses are in a soul bond with God at the helm as they work together as a team towards a shared vision as well as higher purpose in their lives. With seduction, one person entices another to stray from their partner and engage in an interaction that heightens sexual arousal. In the barbeque example, Tom did not try to entice Mona sexually because his response was more about trying to make everyone laugh through this awkward social moment. When Tom said: "Mona you rocked my world baby!" it was with whimsical sarcasm because everyone in the interaction knew that he was not sexually aroused when she accidentally brushed the fork up against his arm.

Flirting, can become very toxic in relationships and lead to broken trust issues when spouses engage in interactions that heighten sexual arousal with others outside of the marriage. Some partners normalize these behaviours by following a "hands off rule" which means that if they do not touch other people then they should still be allowed to act-out sexually with others. A common saying is: "I am allowed to look at the menu, but I just can't order the food." This is one way some people in relationships walk the fine line of commitment in their relationships by being sexual as well as flirtatious, but they do not engage in "cheating" or in what marital relationships would be considered adultery. In essence, they can act sexual with others but they agree they will not touch those people.

Actually flirting is not necessarily an innocent action especially when there is a seductive quality. Remember the definition of the term seduction has two very important verbs which

I Didn't Mean For This To Happen

include _entice_ to _stray_ from right behaviour through interactions that heighten sexual arousal. A husband and wife can seduce each other into being sexually aroused, but this is within the confines of a marital bond blessed by God so this is morally appropriate or right behaviour. With inappropriate flirting, people entice to stray through interactions heightening sexual arousal with others outside of the marriage. In fact, such action is a betrayal to the commitment of marriage. Let's examine how seemingly harmless sexualized interactions with others lead to broken trust in marriages.

Visual Scans, Sexual Jokes and Wrestling

Eighty-percent of how we communicate as human beings is through body language. Therefore we as people are attuned to each other's facial expressions, tones of voice, mannerisms, posture, and so on. We not only hear what is being said to us with words, but we also read into what people are saying through their body language. Some individuals are highly sexualized and they will stare at others in an attempt to check-out their body parts. Such people are having sexualized thoughts and becoming aroused as they stare at other individuals' bodies. An example would be the man who is listening intently to a woman speaking but is focused on staring at her breasts while she is talking.

Such visual scans are included in the ways that people act-out sexually. The problem that occurs in marital relationships is that when one spouse is staring at others in a sexualized manner, they are diminishing the value or worth of their marital partner. Sexualized spouses who "check-out" or "scan" other people outside of the marriage are violating the sanctity of marriage because they are sending out signals to others that are enticing or inviting straying actions regardless of whether their intention is to commit adultery (act upon these behaviours) or not.

Cathy Patterson-Sterling

Some people flirt or sexually scan other people because they are hoping that once they send out these sexual signals that recipients of these sexually aroused glances will reciprocate and send back similar welcoming messages charged with sexual energy. These partners who initiate sexual scans or flirting with others outside of the marriage often do so in an attempt to fuel their own egos by convincing themselves that the reciprocation of these messages is a sign that they are indeed valuable or sexually-wanted by others. Married people do not need to be sending sexual signals to people outside of their marriages. When couples have God at the center of their marital relationships and they are having a spouse to share a future with in union, husbands as well as wives should not need to send sexual signals to others outside of the marriage in order to fill up their own egos that need praise or attention.

Even while stating the obvious that flirting with others outside of marriage can be dangerous, I have personally witnessed Christian married couples acting-out sexually with others outside of the marital bond. Such behaviours are carried out with the sense of being playful as people share sexual jokes, send out sexually-inviting messages, and engage in physical wrestling. I have been to social events whereby a wife comes up and gently kicks or pretends to knock over another person's husband. This same husband then retaliates by placing the woman into a head-lock and a wrestling, pin-down match ensues. All of this behaviour is in the name of being "playful" and yet two people who are not even married to each other are rolling around on the ground together. In this same scenario, a friendship blossoms between the man and woman. Then as this friendship progresses, she confides to the man that she is not very happy in her marriage. The man takes on a rescuing role and boosts her self-esteem by telling her how valuable she is and that her husband just does not appreciate her much

I Didn't Mean For This To Happen

at all in this marriage. Before long, boundaries become further blurred because the woman depends on this man as a source that fuels her ego and makes her feel better about herself. This man helps the woman to feel desirable and loved again. The problem is that this woman is somebody else's wife!

Tossing Your Spouse Under The Bus

There are many ways that people justify their flirtatious behaviours. Some people will say that they have a lot of love in them so it is a natural part of their personality to flirt with others. Often men I have worked with as clients will say that they are just a "typical guy" who has a high sex drive and that they are very masculine so as a result they think about sex hundreds of times a day. As a result, such men justify that over time they are bound to flirt because they are charged with sexual energy and such behaviours come naturally.

What flirting spouses need to realize is that when they are sexually acting-out towards others outside of the marriage, they are violating trust in their relationships. Think of marriage as a bus heading in a certain direction which is the shared vision of the future for the marital relationship. There is a sanctity of the marital bond because it has been blessed by God. When a spouse entices someone outside of the marriage to stray through interactions of a sexually-arousing nature (even if it is just plain flirting), they are turning their backs on their marital partners and what would be more commonly referred to on a metaphorical level as "tossing their loved one under the bus." This may seem like an extreme view, but in this dynamic marital partners are part of a team that keep negativity and intrusive forces outside of the sanctity of their marriage. With flirting on a seductive level, the spouse participating in these actions is switching sides of the team and is engaging in sexually-charged interactions with another outside of the marriage regardless of whether touching is involved or not.

Flirting is a "signal behaviour" which means that seductive flirters send out messages (through their body language) that they are sexually-attracted to others. In many instances, these signals may be laughed off or not reciprocated by individuals outside of the marriage. But what if these signals are returned and spouses find others who are sexually interested in them also? For example, Reg is always telling other women that they are beautiful and that their husbands should appreciate them more as he scans his eyes over them while showing off a seductive grin. Some women may feel uncomfortable, others repulsed, and then there are females who may find such attention not only flattering but inviting as well. Rather than Reg standing beside his wife in honour as well as integrity, he is choosing to satisfy his instant needs for gratification without caring about anyone else's feelings. Reg is "trolling" or "fishing" for seductive attention from other women so that he can feel more attractive, masculine, as well as powerful.

Spouses of flirting partners are devalued and lowered in worth because through sexually acting-out the people are meeting their ego needs out of the confines of the marriage. There is nothing honourable about communicating and sending messages with others that relates to sexual value. Spouses do not need to know through flirting that various associates or friends find them desirable and want to have sex with them.

The result of seductive flirting is broken trust in marriages because individuals create an emotional divide in their relationships when they engage in interactions around sexual arousal with others outside of the marital bond. Partners of flirting spouses feel devalued as well as insecure and they often have the lingering doubt of if and when these flirtations will actually lead to adul-

I Didn't Mean For This To Happen

tery. For example, how can Reg's wife in the above example guarantee that when he is sending out inviting sexual signals to other women that he will not follow through on action and have an affair? Over time, Reg's wife grows in her own insecurity because her husband is meeting his sexual needs for attention outside of the marriage. People who love each other in a marriage blessed by God do not try to make others feel worthless or insecure.

As we continue further along the continuum of flirting, let's examine other sexual behaviours that lead to broken trust in marriages which include on-line sexual chat rooms, phone sex, and cyber affairs through the internet.

Playing In The Shadows With Sexually Acting-Out

Many people justify sexually acting-out outside of their marriages because they are following a supposed "hands-off rule" which means that they convince themselves that they are not technically engaging in inappropriate or adulterous behaviours because they are not touching other people in a sexual manner. With the advent of computers as well as the internet world, inappropriate or even damaging communication outside of marriages has become more common in practice.

All over the internet there are discussion forums whereby people from around the world can log-in on their computers and talk to each other. These forums can relate to particular topics and interests or they can be part of more general chat rooms whereby strangers casually talk to each other. One of the difficulties with computer activities is that there are two very potent factors which include availability as well as anonymity which can impact relationships. In other words, people can go on the computer and connect with all kinds of people (*availability*) and maintain a level of secrecy (*anonymity*) around what exactly they are doing on the computer while also concealing their identities with private e-mail addresses, log-in names, avatars, or call signs. In other words, people can communicate without others knowing their true identities or home locations. The result is that the potential for fantasy exploration with strangers is enormous and people become detached from thinking they will encounter consequences for their actions because after all no one really knows who they are in the first place.

By logging into chat rooms, people can have discussions about sex as well as relationships. There is a façade that builds between participants because they have a sense of connecting with each other and have an illusion of safety because they are in total control of how much they share of themselves or if they will reveal information about their personal identities. As a result, there is a related sense of intrigue, intensity, and excitement because people can discuss forbidden topics or even share their true feelings without any supposed complications or consequences. For example, Sarah from Oklahoma may complain about her husband's lack of intimacy or sexual techniques with Jayson from Thunder Bay, Ontario. He can provide suggestions to her as well as demonstrate compassion for her situation without any consequences occurring. Furthermore, Sarah may not even be Sarah and is instead Floinda from Frankfurt, Germany. Also Jayson might not even be Jayson who boasts about being a tall, adventurous, slim world traveller with a trust fund to spend. Meanwhile, Jayson is really Fred who is short, fat, has never travelled, and works as a Janitor. Also Jayson and Sarah may even feel like they have a special bond of truly understanding each other because each person has particular sexual tastes, enjoys certain fantasies, and likes to get a little "kinky" in the bedroom. In simpler terms, both Jayson and Sarah supposedly understand each other's kink or unique sexual needs.

I Didn't Mean For This To Happen

  Such discussions as well as connections are based on an illusion because neither person has to really share parts of themselves and instead they can discuss as well as build upon through discussion a fantasy world together. Over time, Jayson may even share his fantasy world with Sarah as the two talk openly about what they would like to do to each other if they had a chance. There is no reality or responsibility because neither person places demands on the other and instead they become each other's outlets for escape. When Sarah is arguing with her husband she can feel better knowing that there are men out there like Jayson who would love to ravish her in the bedroom and fulfill every sexual fantasy. Likewise, Jayson (who in reality is Fred) never has to face the fact that his family-life is falling apart due to his lack of communication with his wife and sons. He is emotionally-unavailable, constantly raging, and is completely dissatisfied with his life. Rather than dealing with these issues and growing together as a Christian family blessed by God, Jayson seeks solace in his internet chats or discussions.

  Jayson further escapes into a world of fantasy with Sarah at the center of his obsessions. Her love is unconditional and she understands him completely. In fact, her goal is to please him and over time he concentrates more on her as an escape to his increasing unhappiness in his own life at home. Both Sarah and Jayson feel like they are in a spirit bond because of their deep appreciation of each other. Maybe over time these same people decide that they should meet in person to see if the reality is as good as the fantasy obsession that the two have created together over the internet? Sarah leaves a note for her husband as she anticipates this exciting journey across to the world. She is going to finally meet her true love Jayson. As she departs off of the plane she is ready to consume herself in the excitement of holding another man who truly understands the essence of her heart as well as soul. Sarah gazes across the crowded airport and glances over towards the meeting spot as she sees a short, squat man holding a handful of wilted daisies pacing back and forth. Could this nervous little man really be Jayson her true-love?

Chat rooms and fantasy obsession can serve as the vehicles that cause broken trust in relationships. In the above example, Fred (a.k.a Jayson) convinces himself that he is having harmless fun on the internet because after all he is just talking to another woman. He justifies that he is not touching Sarah and he has the added security of knowing that she is not aware of his real identity. He is able to have a clear differentiation between his home-life with his wife and kids which is separate from his connection to Sarah. The problem is that this connection with Sarah grows as they build a fantasy world together. Rather, than meeting his emotional needs through his wife, Fred is confiding in another woman who now becomes the center of his relationship. God is not at the helm of this marital bond between Fred and his wife and instead the emotional distance grows in Fred's relationship with his spouse. He emotionally shuts-down in his interactions with his wife and kids as he spends more time rushing to the computer to secretly communicate with Floinda (a.k.a Sarah). The intensity as well as excitement of Sarah's messages becomes an intoxicating drug which he slowly mistakes as real intimacy. Fred uses the rush of this communication with Sarah as a source of escape and initiates the process of not only breaking trust with his wife but also exiting his marriage. Furthermore, Fred's relationship with God deteriorates as well as he rationalizes his emotional cyber- affair with Sarah and loses focus of his own spirituality. He needs more and more of Sarah's attention to fuel his ego. She makes him feel special as well as needed. If Fred focuses on his relationship with

God, then he just feels plain guilty as well as shameful about his actions.

Phone Chat Lines

Another way that trust can be broken in relationships is with phone chat lines. With this technology, complete strangers can talk to each other with privacy as well as complete anonymity. As with cyber internet chat rooms, participants can conceal their identities and engage in all kinds of risky conversations. If individuals really feel a connection with each other then they can enter a code and break-off into their own private conversations. Such activities can be particularly scintillating because individuals are not just reading typed text as in cyber chat rooms, but they can hear each other's voices or inflections in tone. Therefore the ability for sexual arousal can become that much more intense as people growl and make sounds at each other. Of course with anonymity, individuals can pretend to be whoever they want as they enhance their own alter-egos or "phone identities." As well, participants can have very intrusive conversations (such as "talking dirty") or discuss topics that would be inappropriate in normal social situations because no one really knows each other and if events become uncomfortable people can just simply hang up the phone. Thus such activities are deemed by many as harmless fun because so long as adults are participating than these phone line chats are consensual.

The difficulty with phone chat lines is that this technology is a vehicle for strangers to sexually arouse each other. With the power of sound people can add noises to their sexually-charged discussions, act-out a conversation around phone sex as they dare each other to take off their clothes, and engage in self-masturbation as they talk about sexual actions. Spouses often justify their behaviours because they are following the "hands-off" principle and are not technically touching other participants of these conversations over the phone.

Trust is broken in marriages whereby spouses are engaging in sexual arousal with others outside of the marital bond. Another huge violation is that spouses know their actions around phone sex are a betrayal to their marital partners and as a result they will often be deceitful by lying or sneaking around so they can have these inappropriate sexually-charged conversations with strangers. This sexual outlet can become particularly exciting because of the sneakiness involved. Often spouses who engage in phone sex with strangers experience an adrenaline rush around the potential of being caught in their actions. This intensity of possibly being caught adds to the thrill as well as exhilaration of such behaviours. The adrenaline rush can serve as a high particularly as people consider the fact that their families are sound asleep in other rooms of their houses while they are on the phone sexually acting-out and "being naughty" with strangers. Sometimes participants of phone sex activities make themselves even more aroused because they embellish this secret or "dark side" of their characters knowing that they have a squeaky clean image as well as position of responsibility in their regular social worlds. Such individuals delight in knowing that they have an exciting, sexual or even deviant side of themselves that they keep as a secret.

As a result of this arousing fear of being caught, some people will be more reckless or even careless in their behaviours so they stay on the phone talking sexually even when their spouses are awake in other rooms. Over time, some spouses with this fantasy obsession of being sexually charged with strangers via phone sex become sloppy in concealing their deceitful behaviours because of the thrill playing with the negative consequences of their spouses possibly learning about these activities. Spouses who do learn of

I Didn't Mean For This To Happen

their partners' inappropriate sexual behaviours often feel an added level of betrayal because of how easily these behaviours were detected. Some wives feel like their husbands are purposefully trying to punish them by acting-out in obvious ways and being caught. Often a wife in such a situation will say to me: "I knew we were having problems communicating, but I did not realize that he was beginning to hate me and did this on purpose to destroy me!" Partners who are acting-out sexually are rarely trying to punish their spouses and are instead caught up in the thrill of fantasy obsession behaviours. In most of these cases partners deeply love their spouses and families, however, they are playing with the negative consequences of potentially being caught because they are heightening the intensity of such experiences.

Another problem with fantasy obsession is that there is a process of *desensitization*. Such obsessions are insatiable and the excitement of these behaviours can wear off quickly. In other words, people need more intensity in order to reach some level of satisfaction or contentment. As a result, sexually-charged interactions are often progressive in nature. Therefore spouses often need more intensity so their sexual acting-out behaviours escalate. With phone sex, people are sexually aroused out of a sense of being naughty or doing things that are against the norm. In order to satisfy sexual desires, over time talking to strangers in a sexual way becomes boring. The thrill of speaking about sex with others outside of the marital bond has passed and now spouses who act-out sexually with others may need an entirely new medium in which to explore the sensations of sexual arousal. This is the reason why people who sexually act-out may send each other naked pictures of themselves or watch each other through web cams. With the advent of high speed technology and social media the consequences of getting caught are instant and the potential for public humiliation is high.

Another way people act-out along the sexual continuum is with pornography.

Pornography

Pornographic images are scattered throughout the internet and some people even join clubs or associations so they can share specific files of pornographic images. Individuals may even have a sense of camaraderie as they meet others on-line who share similar sexual appreciations or "kinks." Some people have fetishes around feet or like to be voyeurs so they share pictures as well as video footage of strangers engaging in sexual acts together. The danger with pornography involves this type of **desensitization** as well whereby certain sexual images are no longer satisfying over time. Therefore some people feed the adrenaline rush of sexual arousal by trying to gain more of a realistic experience of an escalating nature. For example, people may grow tired of watching static photos of naked body parts so they go to websites whereby there are moving images of people having sex together. Part of the thrill of fantasy obsession is that people have control over a world whereby they have the key (with the click of a mouse on a computer) into a socially taboo and forbidden world.

Control is a very strong theme in fantasy obsession and the ultimate taboo around control is to sexualize on to images of young people. Teenagers or even children represent innocence and in a world of fantasy part of the thrill is visualizing "stealing someone's innocence" and having them dependent on learning from masters the techniques involved in creating as well as maintaining sexual arousal. Therefore in pornography, images of young girls in cheerleading outfits, private school uniforms, or French maid costumes are very popular. In these fantasies, men who are filled with sexual

I Didn't Mean For This To Happen

knowledge help access young cheerleaders', school girls', or even maid's hidden sexual desires. During such fantasies, men are in control while corrupting the innocence of young women as they introduce them into a world of complete sexual indulgence or ecstasy. The ultimate taboo would be images of children being molested and introduced into sex. There is a power differential whereby the men are older, skilled, and knowledgeable (the mentors or masters) and the young teenagers or children are disciples. In more extreme cases, virgins are held as prizes and conquering the innocence of virginity and having sex with a virgin is a fantasy image.

This same power differential or imbalance in power as well as control is in other types of fantasies which may include rape scenes whereby a man steals the innocence as well as trust from a woman who does not consent and then is overpowered by the man's strength. In some fantasy images the overpowered woman submits and by being dominated she is surprisingly aroused on a sexual level as she begins to enjoy this treatment. The dominant man has secretly unlocked her desires of being conquered and has made this innocent female who is "good" enjoy being "dirty" or "bad." Finally, there are three way fantasies whereby men are engaged in sex with two women who are lesbians. The men in these scenes are so potent or powerful that the women who normally enjoy having sex with each other are so drawn to the man's sexual magnetism that they abandon their homosexual interests and aim to please the man sexually. In most pornography scenes the climatic ending involves men ejaculating on to women's faces or other body parts as a symbol of complete control as well as domination. Over time visual pornographic images are no longer exciting so people escalate to interactive sex sites.

Cathy Patterson-Sterling

Trust is broken in relationships whereby spouses are looking at pornography. Such actions are not harmless. A huge problem is that people who fuel fantasy obsession with pornographic images run the risk of damaging their marriages. Such people become *sexualized* on to objectified images (body parts and sexual actions). The focus in on the orgasm and being consumed in sexual arousal rather than to appreciate love, tenderness, or intimacy in a marital bond blessed by God.

In pornography, images become an outlet for sexual release. As a result, real sexual relations between husbands and wives can become tainted as partners who view pornography can transfer this same focus on orgasms to their spouses. Love-making then becomes a perfunctory function around "getting off" or being satisfied sexually rather than focusing on the intimacy of closeness. People who become dependent on pornographic images condition themselves to focus on orgasms and the potential is for their marital partners to be treated as a vehicle or outlet for sexual release. The result is that spouses of people who focus on fantasy obsession with pornography often feel used as well as *objectified* because they believe their partners provide attention mainly by requesting sex. Such spouses of pornography-dependent individuals do not feel valued as human beings and are treated as if they are there to serve just a sexual function.

Some husbands will justify this sexual focus by convincing themselves that their wives should feel blessed to be getting so much attention sexually. The problem is that when men are *conditioned* on to pornographic sex images, they often lose sight of the inherent human value of their wives. Instead, such men appear to be "under a sexual spell" as they reach out and grab the body parts of their wives. These men are focused on their own needs and with intensity convince their wives to have sex with them.

I Didn't Mean For This To Happen

In these situations, men are not appreciative of their wives' value and are focused instead on body parts. Therefore women often feel used because their husbands are reaching and/or grabbing at them as if they are pieces of meat. Furthermore, in these cases men are neglectful of the situational timing involved. Such men want their instant gratification needs for sex fulfilled regardless of whether their wives are busy, not feeling well, or are emotionally-upset. This type of disregard for the wives' emotions becomes part of the violating effects.

Furthermore, some men may push their wives to become more sexually adventurous because they want to emulate the behaviours they see in the pornographic images. The problem is not that men's wives are prudish, but rather there is an insatiable quality in these interactions. Often husbands who are dependent on pornography are not easily satisfied and when they have sex with their wives they want even more or in many cases they pressure these women into engaging in increasingly intense sexual interactions. For example, many fantasy obsessed men are not content to have sex once and a while as they pressure their wives to be sexual multiple times a day. If such women submit, then these men place increasing demands on their wives to act-out fantasies or explore more adventurous sexual positions and rituals. Some men use guilt tactics like appearing hurt and not talking so that their wives feel bad if they do not relent to the sexual advances. The problem that wives in these situations encounter is that fantasy driven interactions are insatiable and even if such women give in to their husbands' sexual desires these men are never content and just push for more sexual interactions. Trust is easily broken in such relationships because women in these situations feel like their needs are completely disregarded as their husbands just keep trying to fuel the bottomless pit of sexual arousal by using their wives as objects for sexual release or more crudely as "fantasy pound pillows."

In other instances, men who are driven by fantasy obsession with pornography may even lose interest sexually in their wives. Over time these men become sexualized on to body part images in which they are able to masturbate thus being in control of the timing, frequency, and type of sexual arousal they experience. Some men find bargaining with their spouses for sexual attention a hassle and they do not have the patience for their wives' reluctance to trying to intensify sexual interactions by being more adventurous. Also these same men may feel guilty for feeling unfulfilled with their wives because once they have sex with them they just want to have even more sexual interactions so the arguing that ensues can become tiring. If men leave it to themselves to satisfy their own sexual pleasures, then they do not have to interact with their wives. As a result, many fantasy obsessed men start to lose sexual interest in their wives and especially with the process of ***desensitization***, they may not even be able to sexually perform with their wives because they have been sexualized on to intense sexual situations that are only available through pornography.

Trust is often broken in these circumstances as well because such men become emotionally unavailable to their wives because they need more intensity through pornography to satisfy their sexual urges and as a result the women of these men may feel rejected or even abandoned. Some women will blame themselves for their husband's lack of interest in them. As result, it is not uncommon for wives of fantasy obsessed men to become insecure as they wonder what they have done wrong to make their husbands so sexually disinterested? The more these women are abandoned emotionally, the more they may try to engage sexually with their husbands and with each rejection they may feel increasingly de-

I Didn't Mean For This To Happen

fective as human beings. Such women do not realize that their husbands are quite simply sexualized on to pornographic images and that this is not an indicator that these wives have done anything wrong at all. In marital bonds blessed by God, husbands are not there to be in complete control as they dominate as well as objectify their wives so women have not provoked their husbands into sexually-acting out. Instead, men use fantasy obsession as an outlet for escape and as a way to mood-alter by becoming aroused sexually on an intense and sometimes deviant level. Wives do not force husbands towards the temptation of pornographic images. Rather, fantasy-obsessed partners need to take the responsibility of their own choices of using this escape outlet of pornography.

Sometimes men will use excuses for their attachment to pornography by blaming their wives for not satisfying their sexual needs. Women can easily become scapegoats in these dynamics. Husbands can use the convenience of blaming their wives as a way to alleviate their own guilt around their behaviours. For example, if George suggests that Sheila (his wife) is not accessible for sex and that she regularly is denying his needs then he can justify his obsession with pornography. George can stay in this rut of using fantasy obsession as an outlet for excitement and mood-altering through sexually arousing images without worrying about the impact of his behaviours on Sheila because of course she is to blame for his actions. In reality, George needs to take responsibility for his role in the marital breakdown because rather than justifying his behaviours, he should become responsible and work through any issues he has in the marriage. Instead, he escapes from any emotional complications or tensions through his actions of masturbating with pornography. The emotional divide between George and Sheila increases because for George collecting more intense sexual images on the computer becomes a greater priority than being a loving husband or having a marriage whereby God is at the center of this relationship.

Cyber Sex Affairs

In order to satisfy a level of sexual intensity, some people wish to participate in sexual actions while still remaining safe as well as anonymous. This way such individuals do not have to risk the negative consequences of getting caught because they can maintain their anonymity by using log-in names, avatars, or call signs. This way they are both in control of maintaining their anonymity and can even in many occasions direct the actions of what events are occurring on their computer screens. With the technology of web cams, people can be sexually interactive while still maintaining the "hands-off rule" of not physically touching the people they are interacting with on the screen. By using web cams, individuals can enter computer sites and view strangers. With the ability to log in, these same people can type in requests for strangers to take off clothing items or even engage in certain sexual behaviours such as touching themselves as well as playing with sex toys and so on. The lure of web cam sex is that people can feel powerful by having the ability to make others obey their commands. Individuals can also engage in sexual peep shows whereby they pay money in order to see other people strip naked. There is also an opportunity for people to even engage in real time one on one masturbation as they act as both voyeur (doing the watching) and exhibitionist (doing the sexual acting-out). Such options are accessible because individuals can connect with this world through the click of a computer button rather than taking the risk of being detected by walking through seedy red light districts filled with prostitutes as well as adult pornography stores.

Physical Affairs Without Emotions

As discussed previously, some people justify sexually acting-out outside of the marital bond through the *"hands-off rule"* because they are not technically touching others during their sexual arousal. People who have physical affairs (engage in sexual acts on a bodily or touching level) with others often justify their behaviours through an *"emotions-off rule."* Such individuals believe they are protecting the sanctity of marriage because they are not in love with or emotionally-connected to the people they sexually act-out with on a physical level. These people who engage in physical affairs often believe that love and sex can be two entirely different actions that have nothing to do with each other. Men in these situations often claim that they love their wives as well as families and yet they still act-out sexually with people outside of the marital bond.

Anonymous Infidelity

With the progression of technology, sexual intercourse and even oral sex with strangers while still concealing a personal identity or information is more readily available. Individuals can link to sites and log in their GPS (Global Positioning Systems) attached to their phones as they easily locate others who wish to participate in similar sexual activities. Also if individuals are wanting to find other people in their local communities who wish to meet to engage in sexual activities, they can just go to local websites that display buy and sell sections. Rather than searching for used furniture, people post ads enticing others into having sex with no attachments or complications. The fact that these strangers do not know each other and are clear about not wanting to establish a relationship of any kind means that they can delude themselves into believing that such actions are harmless because this sex is consensual. In fact, such activities are often referred to as "play" whereby the consenting adults become "play partners" with each other. The larger problem is that such behaviour is a violation of the sacred marriage bond blessed by God and these risky actions can lead to absolute marital devastation.

The lure of these activities is the exciting thrill that people can experience through the anticipation of being sexual with people they do not know. Of course the obvious problem is that spouses who engage in anonymous infidelity are placing their partners at risk for diseases and there is a major betrayal of trust through these actions. The two strangers may be consenting to these activities, however, the spouses of these individuals are not provided with the option of knowing the reality that the people they trust as well as love and have families with are having sex with individuals outside of the marriage.

Another way that people engage in anonymous infidelity is by going to men's massage parlours or bath houses. Escorts who have the façade of acting as masseuses provide sexual or "sensual massages" which can include sexual intercourse, manual masturbation, as well as oral sex that come as additional services to the massage. Some husbands justify their actions because they have no emotional attachments to the "masseuses" and after all they are paying for a service.

Prostitution

Some people justify purchasing the services of escorts or prostitutes as one of the oldest professions in the world. The rationalization is that men with large sexual appetites cannot expect to be satisfied by their wives especially if such women are unavailable for sex since they are menstruating, pregnant, menopausal, and so on. Therefore payment for sexual services is a perfunctory function with no emotional attachments involved because the female prostitutes are just performing a service for sexual release.

Another lure of prostitution is that fantasy obsessed men can meet their needs for power as well as control by ordering another

I Didn't Mean For This To Happen

human being to perform sexual functions for payment. Some men will even objectify female prostitutes by considering them to have no real human value because they are "ho's", "hookers", "sluts", and so on. Therefore such men resolve any guilt they might feel about betraying the marital bond because they have no emotional attachment to what they classify as lower level street workers who degrade themselves through prostitution.

Some men become a little more involved with prostitutes on an emotional level while still maintaining complete control as well as anonymity. These husbands take pity on prostitutes who they view as "dirty damsels in distress." Therefore such men demonstrate compassion through a lens of moral superiority. Often men with a rescuing complex believe there is a huge divide in social status between themselves and women of the streets and in order to prove their superior status they will ask these ladies questions about their lives. As the street women describe their difficulties as well as struggles with their oppressive pimps and so on, men with rescuing issues will give them money. Such financial funds, however, are mere pittance because the men's motivations are to show off that they have money as well as resources. This way the men can alleviate any guilt they may feel by purchasing sex from street workers while also fuelling their own egos as they try to demonstrate that they have a higher social status in which they can spend money easily. A common saying would be to "toss the dog a bone." Some men "toss" money at prostitutes (without valuing them as human beings) just to show off the fact they have money in the first place.

These same husbands may then return to their wives and act doting as well as affectionate as they purchase "guilt gifts" in order to make up for their transgressions with prostitutes. Some husbands will put on enormous public displays of affection as they purchase elaborate gifts for their wives which are revealed in front of various friends and family. Surrounding people may even be envious of the marriage these husbands and wives exhibit. In reality, however, these husbands are just alleviating their guilt around their secret activities with prostitutes. Such men justify that their wives are somehow benefiting from these hidden deceptions with paid street workers because at least they receive gifts as well as public displays of attention.

When wives find out about this betrayal, trust in the relationship is not only devastated, but these women become enraged as well as confused that the husbands they love could be so attentive and also engage in adultery with paid sex trade workers. Many wives wonder how they could have husbands with such "Jekyll" (good) and "Hyde" (bad) personalities? These wives also experience an intensified emotional crisis as well because they now have to begin the journey of getting tested for sexually transmittable diseases as well as HIV. This is not the type of reality they bargained for when they made the commitment to the Christian marital vow that was blessed by God as well as witnessed by so many friends and family.

Not all adultery and betrayal is non-emotional and just about sexual acting-out. Sometimes feelings are involved in physical affairs with the result being that trust in marriages is completely obliterated.

Physical Affairs With Emotional Attachment

Some people will commit adultery on their spouses and there are feelings combined with their actions. Such individuals are not just acting-out sexually, but they end up establishing sexual relationships on a feeling level with people outside of the marital bond. The lure of physical affairs exists because individuals often mistake intensity with intimacy. People who are susceptible to

I Didn't Mean For This To Happen

having affairs appreciate the attention that they get from others outside of the marriage. For example, Darius may feel like he is getting on with age and his interactions with his wife are all about responsibilities as she hands him a never-ending series of "Honey to do" lists in which is expected to fix the garage door, mow the lawn, paint the side of the house, clear the gutters and so on. Also, Darius may feel like his children who are teenagers now are "unappreciative money-spending machines" who just keep asking for more money. Darius has created a world for himself whereby he does not communicate about his pressures but would rather be nostalgic about the good old days when he was young, virile, and sexually-desirable. Now he is just handed a list of chores. When Darius encounters Louann (a woman from his work), she brings out the free-spirited side of himself. She laughs at his jokes, bats her eyelashes at him when he makes sexual inferences, and just genuinely appreciates him. In order to feel better about himself, Darius would rather spend time around Louann than his nagging wife. Louann's attention helps to fuel Darius' ego. When Darius is around Louann he feels an intense rush of excitement which is a welcome relief from the burdened life he has created for himself in his mind.

As time progresses, Darius becomes more attached to the sensations he experiences while being in Louann's company. Furthermore, Louann is in a similar position in that she feels like her husband is not meeting her emotional needs since he is always busy working all of the time. Darius and Louann begin to believe that they have an intense connection that is shared by only the two of them. Both individuals think this intensity is really intimacy and a deep understanding because their interactions with each other come so easily. Darius feels like he can be at peace and be free to act-out his real self without any sense of responsibility. In fact,

Darius and Louann are building a fantasy world together that they mistake as reality. Each person is moving further into a violation that goes against their marriages with their spouses. With each touch, both Darius and Louann experience a climactic moment. They both think this excitement is a sign that they are bonded together as soul mates who have a mutual deep understanding. In reality, the secrecy as well as excitement about possibly getting caught in their affair is the adrenaline rush they are both craving. Unfortunately, they both mistake this thrill as a sign of true love. This great bubble world they create together will burst once they settle into a relationship and demand responsibilities out of each other. The problem is, however, that in the process two marriages and families will be completely devastated.

Of the different types of trust that can be broken in relationships, sexual acting-out and affairs are only part of an entire gamut of deceptions. Some people will betray trust in their marriages through abuse of chemicals or the self-destructive use of mood-altering substances.

Playing In The Shadows With Chemicals

There are many people in our society who drink alcohol socially, and then there are others that use drugs on an experimental or what could be viewed as a recreational level. In marriages, spouses can not only break trust in their relationships by acting out on a sexual level, but they can also negatively impact their marriages by abusing mood-altering substances like prescription medicine, alcohol, or with illicit (non-legal) drugs like marijuana and so on. When individuals initially experiment or socially use alcohol and/or drugs, their intentions may be to experience pleasurable feelings. The difficulty, however, is that if people become dependent on these substances then they can use alcohol and/or drugs as a method of coping in life. For example, some people do not deal with stress very well so they will drink alcohol like wine or beer as a way to make these overwhelming feelings go away. Over time, however, these same people can develop a dependency on mood-altering and as a result they do not deal with their problems because they are drinking or drugging away their feelings.

Marriages can be severally impacted by substance abuse because the spouse who is drinking or using drugs begins to develop an attachment to these substances and they become protective over their new relationships with the alcohol or drug. In fact, the mood-altering substances can provide instant relief so people are often willing to put up with arguments or criticisms from their spouses around their drinking or drugging because the chemical they are using provides the necessary relief or escape from life that they believe they need in order to cope over time. Some spouses will even describe their partners' relationships with alcohol or drugs as a type of "affair" because substance abusing people will often lie, be secretive, manipulate, and sneak around in order to use their drugs or alcohol. This type of lying as well as secrecy is common in real affairs with adults outside of the marriage. The problem with substance abuse, however, is that the "affair-like" behaviours of lying and so on relate to chemicals and other people outside of the marriage are not necessarily involved. Instead, people who abuse substances will disappear for hours or even days at a time, isolate themselves, make excuses to be around others who drink or use drugs, or act in self-destructive ways by driving impaired and so on.

Trust is broken in marriages where substance abuse is involved for many reasons. One problem with substance dependency is that people who abuse alcohol or drugs begin to experience negative consequences for their actions and in spite of these problems, they continue to resolve their issues with even more alcohol or drugs. For example, Frank is overwhelmed by all of his work responsibilities and he is not communicating about his stress with his wife. When he comes home, he reaches for a beer and settles himself on to the couch as he watches television. He is not interested in discussing the quality of his day at work and he believes he is just de-stressing or unwinding from a long work shift. As the evening progresses, Frank consumes a few more beer as he glazes over from the effects of the alcohol and then falls asleep. Frank ignores the emotional distance between himself and his wife as he rationalizes that she is always nagging and making demands of him. When Frank stumbles from the effects of his drinking, he blames his wife for not cleaning up the house properly so the result is that he ends up tripping on his slippers. In reality, Frank was under the influence of alcohol and this is the reason that he fell to the floor. Over time, Frank continues to find solace in beer.

The difficulty with substance dependency, however, is that the negative consequences from abusing alcohol and drugs continue to increase and do not automatically disappear as a pattern begins to emerge. Now Frank is becoming sick from his beer consumption and does not show up for work. Rather than dealing with this emerging problem, Frank continues to follow the solution he sees for his problems which is to just drink more alcohol. As he progresses with abusing alcohol, he may suffer more consequences such as increased arguments with his wife and the possibility that he may receive disciplinary action from his company for not showing up to work. When Frank does attend work, he makes even more excuses to leave early so that he can drink. Over time Frank learns to disguise his drinking while working which becomes a major safety issue since he is a crane operator.

Substance dependency is very problematic because individuals who are abusing substances often do not realize the impact of

I Didn't Mean For This To Happen

their actions right away. Rather than dealing with issues, people who abuse mood-altering substances try to seek more relief in the alcohol and/or drugs. When such individuals are faced with problems, they rationalize or justify their behaviours in order to maintain their relationship with these chemicals. The result is frequently an emotional divide in marriages as individuals who abuse substances often lie, cheat, steal, or deny issues so that they can drink their alcohol or use drugs. As a result, people with substance abuse issues or even dependency likely need the outside help of support meetings, counsellors and possibly a treatment program because they may believe the lies they tell themselves as they minimize the impact of their drinking and/or drugging behaviours.

Some people act out sexually, others with chemicals, and then there are also individuals who spend money on a frivolous or even self-destructive level. The result is that trust in marriages can easily be broken in not just matters of the heart but in issues that involve money.

Playing In The Shadows With Money And Spending

For many people spending money can become quite the exhilaration especially with the excitement involved in purchasing new items. Trust in marriages, however, can become easily broken when one spouse satisfies their needs for instant gratification by personally spending money that relates to the priorities or goals of the shared vision for a couple. For example, some people have joint bank accounts and they trust that when they have to pay off debts that there will be funds available. Trust is easily broken when one partner takes that money whether it be from a joint account or part of an agreed upon investment fund and spends these finances on personal as well as frivolous items that are not highly valued or needed by the couple.

Part of the reason why trust can be broken is that partners who compulsively spend money are not considering the needs of their spouses. Also with such erratic spending habits, one partner can put an entire couple into financial peril. In Christian marriages, people have common goals with God at the center of their relationships. When one partner compulsively spends money they are abandoning the teamwork of the marriage and are more interested in satisfying their own selfish interests regardless of the other spouse's feelings.

Spending serves a purpose as type of "feel good experience" whereby people can distract from their real feelings and create happiness instantly as they revel in the excitement of their newly purchased items. The problem is that this type of happiness is not sustainable and has instead an insatiable quality. Individuals who spend in a way to feel better are rarely satisfied because this happy sensation is temporary. Often people need more and more items to try to fill up the emptiness that they commonly feel inside.

Compulsive spending has a self-destructive element which is often referred to as "buyer's remorse." This means that individuals may purchase items and be so caught up in the moment that they neglect examining any longer term implications of their actions. For example, Hilary may buy the amazing new car with the leather interior and all of the latest technology without considering the responsibility or impact on her budget of making those monthly payments on a brand new high grade vehicle. Instead, she was so caught up in the rush and excitement to see if she would be pre-approved for financing that she thought that the approval that came in was an indication that she should actually purchase the new car. When the reality sinks in, Hilary may feel regretful for her actions as she comprehends that these new payments will

I Didn't Mean For This To Happen

completely impact her budget for her family. She had not considered the impact of this decision on her children or husband.

Some people will gamble as a way of compulsively spending money. This habit may be in the form of casino style games, on-line poker or slots, as well as investing in the stock market. There is a rush or excitement involved in spending finances with the potential to make even more money. The problem is that when people begin to experience a depletion of money, rather than stopping their behaviours of spending they start to "chase" the losses which means that they use more money to try to recuperate their losses. For many individuals, this behaviour of "chasing losses" is the beginning of a downward spiral in which they end up losing even more money than they ever invested in the first place. Such losses can significantly impact couple's financial savings which results in not only broken trust but in some cases financial ruin.

Playing In The Shadows With Work Addiction and Impact Ego

There are several pay-offs for extreme working which I refer to as the "ACE Effect." People who are focused intensely on work can feel like they are A-accomplishing great feats, C- feeling a sense of purpose as well as control, and E- escaping into work projects. Such individuals can live in their "bubble-worlds", whereby they are at the center of their own important activities. With constant ringing cell phones and everyone demanding their attention as well as time, such individuals can feel important or even like specialized masters of their own domains or work fields.

This rush of excitement of meeting deadlines, project details, or creating a tremendous impact on others can become a safe place of escape. For example if the children are whining and the spouse is nagging, then individuals can seek solace in their work projects. While working, reality becomes finite as well as focused on the task at hand. There are no loud noises, interferences, or emotional demands while individuals immerse themselves into their work schedules. Furthermore, people can ruminate or obsess about details related to projects as they escape into this time-intensive outlet called work. Over time work can become a relief from living. Some individuals even justify their work obsessions because they hand over large pay checks which their families appreciate. Accomplished people who are obsessed with work can justify their extreme work hours by focusing on the money they are able to provide to their families without closely examining the reality that they are emotionally-vacant in their relationships. Impact ego occurs when people are over-working because of their motivations to bolster their ego through the "impacts" they are having by influencing others or doing good work for the benefit of others. These motivations are fuelled by vain self-glory and as a way for people to boost their egos.

Trust is broken in marriages where one spouse is obsessed with work. The foundation for families is not built upon pay checks and love as well as true affection cannot be purchased. Families may enjoy the large sums of money associated with extreme jobs that consume time, however, they are also missing out on emotionally-fulfilling relationships with individuals who are always working. Furthermore, people who are obsessed with work often conserve most of their energies for their jobs while leaving very little quality emotional time for their families. Such individuals may rationalize that they take time to go on outings with their loved ones, however, when they do so they are mentally preoccupied with work details or they are constantly answering ringing cell phones while they have conversations related to their jobs.

Spouses on the receiving end of relationships with work-obsessed people can feel emotionally-abandoned. Accomplished individuals who are so focused on work may surrender their entire identities to their jobs or even their higher callings. In fact such people become "walking-talking resumes" who talk only about their accomplishments or about the people who they are helping. These individuals can over time be one-dimensional. Inside of themselves, these same people may feel like they are following God's will for their lives but the reality is that they are meeting their needs for self-esteem and so on by giving all of themselves to their work responsibilities. At home, such people often act like empty shells collapsed into exhaustion sitting in front of television sets unresponsively flicking through channels with no connection to their families. Other individuals may even have a ritual whereby they "retire to their dens" or home offices as they remain glued to their computers rather than interacting with their loved ones.

In the final group of behaviours that can lead to broken trust in marriages, there is a power imbalance between spouses whereby one partner tries to maintain superiority or control over the other person in the form of emotional or perhaps even physical abuse.

Playing In The Shadows With Manipulations And Control

The term abuse specifically means to mistreat or treat badly. A more elaborate definition is: "pattern of behaviour in which physical violence or emotional coercion is used to gain power or control in the relationship." With abuse, there is a power differential which means that one person makes themselves appear bigger or more superior by acting in a way to make the other individual severally diminished in value as being inferior. Such abusive actions can be completed by a person verbally or accomplished by drastically withdrawing emotional attention in an attempt to punish someone else.

Withdrawing Attention or Affection

Sometimes people will try to control each other rather than communicate. Therefore if someone does something that another person does not like then the offended individual will withdraw their attention which is known as "the silent treatment." This interaction is common when people have arguments with each other as one partner then reacts to the disagreement by emotionally shutting-down and refusing to speak. Although, this way of coping is not always the most responsible or mature behaviour, such a reaction does not always lead to broken trust in relationships.

An emotional divide can be created in marriages whereby one spouse punishes the other when they do not get their own way in issues. For example, Lewis does not like being confronted by his wife Tira. If she asks him where he is going, when he will be back, or any other details then he becomes angry and will not talk to her. Over time Tira learns that if she wants to get Lewis' attention then she needs to be tentative and approach him for his approval which means never placing pressure on him to be accountable. In this relationship, Lewis comes and goes from the house as he pleases and if Tira ever questions him around his behaviours, then he stops speaking to her for long periods of time. In this way Lewis is actually acting abusive on an emotional level because he severally diminishes her value to the point that she feels threatened or intimidated to ever express her feelings in this relationship. Lewis behaves like an overgrown child who tantrums when he does not get his own way. Furthermore, such withdrawing of attention or affection can also come in the form of raging, name-calling, or using insults (otherwise known as "put-downs.") Tira does not have any equality in this marriage as she constantly censors what she says in order to not upset Lewis. Meanwhile, Lewis is not content to just emotionally withdraw from Tira because he establishes superiority over her and further diminishes her value as a person by calling her stupid and reminding her of all of her mistakes. Trust is completely obliterated in this relationship

I Didn't Mean For This To Happen

because Tira can never feel safe to communicate or to express any signs of intimacy since she is always worried that whatever action she takes will upset Lewis.

Minimizing People's Feelings

Another way that people can break trust in their marriages and use emotions to be abusive is to minimize each other's feelings. For instance, some spouses will argue with each other about whether they should feel certain ways or not. Emotional abuse is possible when one partner severely tries to diminish the other person's value by telling them that they are not entitled to their feelings or perceptions. For example, Trisha feels like her husband Sam does not like her family. Every time she wants to spend time with various family members Sam becomes jealous and claims that she does not love him. Sam is obviously struggling with control as well as jealousy issues. When Trisha tries to talk with Sam about this issue he keeps minimizing her feelings by saying that she is acting silly and that he is not trying to stop her from seeing her family. In fact, whenever Trisha wants to do something or go somewhere Sam interrogates her by asking her all kinds of questions and then he stops talking to her. After an emotional impasse, when she describes her hurt feelings, Sam refuses to take responsibility for his actions. Sam continues to argue with Trisha and discount any of her feelings. Over time Sam escalates by demeaning Trisha and challenges her so much around the value of her feelings that Trisha becomes insecure and begins second-guessing her own perceptions. In this situation, Trisha can never trust Sam to validate her feelings or experiences. Instead, he diminishes her perception and tells her that she is being silly whenever she is bothered by his actions. Trisha knows, however, that if she spends time with her family that Sam will either overwhelm her with the intensity of his jealousy or stop talking to her for a period of time.

Sam holds an unspoken emotional threat over Trisha of acting-out if she sees her family so Trisha believes it is easier to separate herself from her family in order to avoid complications with Sam.

Physical Abuse

With physical abuse, one person asserts dominance over the other through the use of physical threats, intimidation, and also assault. Trust is difficult to maintain in such relationships because the abused spouse is always careful to censor their actions or make sure they do not upset their partner otherwise they may be physically assaulted. The common reason why people stay in relationships whereby there is physical abuse is because they usually believe over time that they are truly causing others to be upset. Therefore rather than setting boundaries so that they are not abused, individuals will work harder to try to ensure they do not "create ripples" or engage in actions that make others angry. Also the lure of staying in such marriages occurs because after the physical violence, there is often a honeymoon period whereby the spouse who assaults their partner is remorseful and acts kind so that the relationship does not end.

Therefore people who are victims of domestic violence will often stay in their marriages after assaults because they believe that the worst events of the events are over and they settle into the momentary kindness (as part of the honeymoon phase) offered by their partners. One major difficulty, however, is that over time the honeymoon phase in the abuse cycle becomes shorter and the abusive partner is less regretful. In some relationships, the honeymoon phase disappears all together with the result being that the partner is just abusive. In such cases, people who are victims of domestic violence stay in these relationships out of fear.

There is an entire gamut or continuum of ways that people can act without integrity in their marriages so that the result is

I Didn't Mean For This To Happen

broken trust. Each deceptive or disrespectful behaviour leads to an eventual emotional divide in marriages. One challenge in healing these relationships is that spouses who are on the receiving end of these deceptions or even betrayals in trust can feel such an all-consuming rage that they struggle to overcome resentments that are necessary to resolve if the marriage is to continue. One way of attending to these resentments is to develop a deeper understanding of these issues. People are off-course from integrity in their relationships as they *play in the shadows of life* and become *lost in the fog of their own unhealthy thinking* along the way.

From Playing In The Shadows To Constructing Buildings In The Shadows Of Life

When *people play in the shadows of life* by participating in lying as well as other *acting-out behaviours*, they experience intensity and any danger signals that they are doing something wrong is perceived as excitement.

Let's explore how we got here so far with the acting out behaviour:

1) The person started playing in the shadow of life by acting-out.
2) The person began a path down a golden trail of delusion through the acting-out.
3) The person started lying to themselves as a way of justifying this acting-out.
4) The person started lying to you as a way to "protect" their acting-out.
5) Warning signs and danger signals were ignored by the person because this sense of danger was interpreted as intensity or excitement.

In the shadows we gain a "feel good" experience and this becomes part of what we will call a *controlled emotional release* or **CER**.

The Controlled Emotional Release (CER)

When people act-out, they build a type of escape life for themselves in their minds as they use the activity or chemical to help themselves "melt away" or escape from problems in life. In this escape life, people choose a **CER** (*controlled emotional release*) that works for them and is guaranteed to do what it is meant to do every time. This CER ("feel good experience") may be with alcohol, prescription drugs, sex, lusting, gambling, on-line gaming, gambling, over-spending of money, emotional-eating, and so on.

The CER serves a purpose and it is the "perceived feel good" of why the person acts-out in the first place. With the CER people are able to "lower the volume of noise of thoughts" in their minds as they "drown out", "numb out", or "block out" stress in their lives. As people experience their own individual CER, they feel like they are melting away in euphoria or pleasure. With some CER's, the "high" they are chasing has since long gone and they have not experienced pleasure for years so as a result they are "chasing the high" of how they used to feel earlier on in their addictions or acting-out behaviors.

With the CER, the activity or chemical starts to take on major importance in people's lives. As a result, individuals begin "organizing" their days around opportunities to have their CER or "feel good experience." Over time the activity or chemical becomes the *"organizing principle"* or most important priority as life just kind of revolves around the activity or chemical. People with compulsions as well as addictions start to slowly check out on an emotional level out of their relationships and they lose their abilities to fulfill responsibilities as effectively because they are

I Didn't Mean For This To Happen

more preoccupied with their CER and the escape life they are building for themselves.

Let's look at the CER in motion with different acting-out behaviours:

CER for lusting

A chemical high in the mind with the rush of endorphins, dopamine, as well as adrenaline through sexual arousal. We create this "high" in our own minds through lust and the result is a rush of excitement as well as anticipation while feeling vibrant or alive in a hyper-aroused way with sexual thoughts.

CER for pornography

Similar to the high of lusting, except that people often "download" the sexual images they see in pornography into their minds so that they can pull out this material through their fantasy minds at any time.

CER for cybersex

Similar to the high of lusting, except that people experience the rush of being naughty, the excitement of possibly being caught, and the rush of reciprocation when someone else participates in the fantasy through talking back about sex over the internet or reciprocating the initiations in some way (for example, sending naked pictures or live images of themselves).

CER for emotional affairs

Similar to the high of lusting except that there is an added "rush" or anticipation of seeing that person (who is the object of affection) and also living in the fantasy state of thinking that this other individual really admires, likes, or adores us. This is much like a game of how close we can become to another person of our attraction and the anticipation of seeing that individual is a chemical elixir in the brain of oxytocin, dopamine, adrenaline, and endorphins.

CER for physical affairs

Similar to the high of lusting, but there is the anticipation of the physical conquest of getting close sexually.

CER for alcohol/prescription drugs

The "high" is the ability to numb out with chemicals.

CER for gambling

The "high" is the sense of winning or beating the odds in a game of mastery or chance.

CER for compulsive spending

The "high" is in the possibility of sorting through, discovering, and then attaining a "must have item" with the process of spending money.

CER for on-line gaming

The "high" is losing yourself or melting away into a virtual fantasy world whereby you have no limitations on your power or influence.

CER for emotional-eating

The "high" is being able to be in control of a good feeling of eating while the rest of the world feels out of control. This is much like a process of filling up the emptiness inside through mood-altering with food by providing a sense of comfort.

Once people lock on to the CER or perceived "feel good" of their acting-out behaviours, they will create the opportunities to act-out by focusing a lot of energy on related activities as part of an *escape life* in their minds. For example, John has a problem with lusting so he purposefully seeks out opportunities whereby he can be around women as he lusts over them and sexualizes them in his mind. Jeremy rushes through his work day so that he can get to the casino to gamble. Mary spends countless hours on-line shopping for her perfect "must have" item as she then goes on spending sprees.

I Didn't Mean For This To Happen

As people pour more energy into their acting-out and CER, they begin the process of constructing buildings or setting up residence in the shadows of life. With *compartmentalized thinking*, people do not think that one area of life will impact another. For example, they live in a "what happens in Vegas stays in Vegas mentality" as they are deluded and do not think that negative consequences for their behaviours will apply to them. Such individuals have started the process of descending not only into the golden trail of delusion, but also the "*fog of unhealthy thinking*."

The Fog Of Unhealthy Thinking

In this *fog of unhealthy thinking* sin is alive and in motion. Also as people lie to themselves, they give themselves all kinds of honorable intentions around how if they were honest that their "fragile" spouses could not handle the truth so they are doing them a favor by keeping secrets. In this *fog of unhealthy thinking*, people also grow with a sense of *victim entitlement* whereby they feel like they have sacrificed so much in life (and are in some ways like a victim being done to by others and taken advantage of) that they now deserve their turn to do what they want through their CER. With victim entitlement, people can justify that they deserve to do anything and that consequences will not apply to them. Ted who has a sex addiction had a sense of victim entitlement as he told his wife that of course he had to use the services of a prostitute because it had been two weeks since they had sex. As a man, he had his needs as well and after all he works very hard to bring home an income to his family!

How Christians Play In The Shadows

Christian people who are on a path of righteousness are not immune to *playing in the shadows of life*. In particular many of these acting-out behaviours thrive in a veil of secrecy. Christian people can preserve their "public image" by looking "godly" or having a strong faith in the presence of others while acting-out with their CER in private without others knowing what they are doing much of the time. Also with lusting, Christians can hide their thoughts as part of a fantasy world in their own minds without openly sharing these details with anyone. The problem is that over time as individuals travel down the *golden trail of delusion*, their acting-out takes over more of their lives and the result is that the emotional train in motion now hits the wall and creates the resulting fall-out or emotional wreckage with broken trust.

Another dangerous component is the process of *desensitization*. When people act-out the "high" that they are chasing with the CER begins to wear off and they need more intensity in order to get that same perceived "feel good" feeling. As a result, lusting is not enough as people want to "act-out" these fantasies. Also with pornography, people require more risky images in order to achieve the same sexual arousal. Shoppers need more variety of items and people who use mood-altering substances like alcohol or drugs need more chemicals as their bodies become immune to previous levels of "feel good." Over time people are drawn away from real life into the pursuit of their "high" with the escape life and the CER. Eventually both worlds (the escape life and real life) collide and then come tumbling down.

Bargaining With The CER

When people act-out with their CER, they begin *bargaining* with their compulsion or addiction. This means that they try to find all the ways of being able to do their activity or habit a "little bit" as they convince themselves that their behaviours are not harming anyone. What people do not realize is that their compulsive habit/activity or addiction is taking up more and more of their lives with the cost being to their relationships. With addiction, people are creating "emotional fall-out" or massive problems

I Didn't Mean For This To Happen

in their lives because of their attachment to their CER and escape life. The result is what is called *emotional wreckage* or damage which may include broken trust in relationships, financial issues, and so forth because people will lie, steal, cheat, and deceive in order to protect their CER in life.

A Review Of How We Got Here

Acting-out behaviour is driven by unresolved emotional issues. Partners do not cause their spouses to "act-out" and instead these deeper unresolved issues likely came with individuals into the marriage and have been long buried. Rather than dealing with emotional issues, people act-out with self-destructive behaviours. This process often looks like:

1) The person started *playing in the shadows of life* by acting-out.
2) The person began a path down a *golden trail of delusion* through the acting-out.
3) The person started lying to themselves as a way of justifying this acting-out.
4) The person started lying to you as a way to "protect" their acting-out.
5) Warning signs and danger signals were ignored by the person because this sense of danger was interpreted as intensity or excitement.
6) The acting-out became more frequent because of the CER (*controlled emotional release*) or "feel good" feelings of the acting-out. The CER became a way of escaping from real life or underlying issues that had never been resolved. The person may have even put more energy into the "acting-out" by having a type of *escape life* in their minds by focusing on their fantasies or find-

ing ways to escape from reality into lusting and other acting-out behaviours.

7) The *fog of unhealthy thinking* descended and the person started believing that it was okay to act-out and with a sense of **compartmentalization** they thought that one part of their life with acting-out would not impact real life or their relationships.

Chapter 3
Now What? Can Broken Trust Be Healed?

We are called to move from *playing in the shadows of life* to putting the shadows into the light of healing before God and as a way to end the lies, deceits, and crazy-making cycles that occur as a result of the acting-out. When trust has been broken in marriages, many couples will wonder what it takes to move toward the road to reconciliation? In particular, hurting parties on the receiving end of the broken trust often wonder if forgiveness is possible, how they can overcome the lies and deceptions, or if healing really is an attainable stage? The details of what occurred during the lies and deceptions in the marriage are not as important as the couple's ability to follow through and maintain the steps of the healing process outlined below. Many marriages have survived pornography, addiction, infidelity, and other major crisis with the end result being that couples have come out better as people through this process. In fact, Christian couples can not only heal from broken trust but also attend to the underlying issues that have existed within the marriage prior to the breaking of the trust. The result is that the broken trust then becomes a catalyst for people to positively grow on deeper emotional levels as well as grow in God's grace closer to the design of who we are meant to be as Christians. Many people who heal from this process also move onward to carry the message of healing forward and help other couples in crisis. But, before we get ahead of ourselves, let's examine closely what it takes to heal from this crash and burn crisis in our lives and marriages.

The Injury

Acting-out parties who have broken trust in marriages with their lies and deceptions must walk through a process called ***attending to the wreckage*** which means that they realize not only the cycle of their "acting out behaviours" but they also truly begin a phase of understanding the impact of their behaviours on other people. People who have pornography and fantasy obsessions or carry out affairs/infidelity may have lots of unresolved emotional issues from earlier in life. Some individuals may have had difficult childhoods, trauma experiences, or other circumstances that have profoundly impacted their emotional functioning even now as adults. Such people will need to work through their issues in therapy while also balancing the restoration journey of their marriages. Just because someone had a difficult childhood or challenges in life does not mean that they receive a free pass to then act-out in their marriages. It is unrealistic for people who have broken trust in their marriages to expect their partners to rise to Olympic feats of forgiveness just because they had a difficult past. For some people with pornography or sexual addictions, they will have to balance the recovery journey of learning sexual purity and freedom from sexual sin while also starting a process of rigorous honesty as well as attending to the wreckage of their past behaviours on their marriages.

The following steps are involved in restoring trust and creating possible reconciliation in relationships. The steps are the door that is opened towards healing. There will be no healing or reconciliation if the person who broke trust does not actively work these steps while balancing their own healing and/or recovery.

The Door To Healing

I Didn't Mean For This To Happen

We will use the metaphor of the door to healing for reconciliation in marriages impacted by broken trust. There are four steps to the reconciliation and healing which may occur with the couple in privacy or in couple's therapy. One of these steps is symbolized by the door knob, and the three other steps are symbolized as the hinges on the door. All four steps are necessary for healing and the rebuilding of trust to occur in marriages.

The Door Knob (Step One) Disclosure:

Perhaps the most important step in healing and reconciliation is *disclosure*. This is the step whereby the person who has broken the trust admits the degree to which trust was broken and shares the necessary details of who, when, where, and what occurred in the lies as well as deceptions of the past. On a metaphorical level, disclosure is like attending to the wound in the marriage and cleaning out the cut or injury except that this is occurring of course on deeper emotional as well as spiritual levels within the marriage. Disclosure must be done properly and the person who has broken the trust must consider carefully what they will disclose. Some individuals will disclose every detail and others will decide to share the overall basic theme of what was occurring in the lies and deceptions. For example, a husband who has committed infidelity ten times may disclose that he has had multiple affairs and then resign himself to sharing what he is prepared to share from the past.

All couples are on their own *healing journeys* and at different stages. Some couples are focused on *stabilization* and they are just coming to terms with the acting-out behaviours and what this all means, other couples have stabilized and they are working through the odd craving or slips while focusing on getting their relationships healthy, and other couples are working on the larger long term changes toward rebuilding intimacy or even more satisfying connections in their relationships. We will examine the issue of disclosure. If you have already completed disclosure, then there is no sense in re-visiting it, but in case all of the facts are not on the table and you are still wondering what it is that you are dealing with then disclosure is a critical first step.

What Is Disclosure And Why Is It Needed?

With the cataclysmic fracture of broken trust that has shot through the center of your relationship, you as a hurting party have suffered an ***emotional injury***. Likely, this experience was one of feeling ***emotionally blindsided*** whereby you may have felt "sideswiped" like this situation came out of nowhere. For some people this is much like an emotional car accident scene and they feel broadsided. Such individuals "may have heard the car screeching in the distance" before actual impact which is the metaphor for the vague awareness of the acting-out behaviours in the distance. For example, some people have a "gut feeling" that their partners are having an affair or acting-out (the screeching of brakes in the distance before impact) just before they discover the truth about the secret escape life.

Now as hurting parties move forward they have to resolve two issues:

1) Attending to the emotional injury. For example, getting safe and re-grouping around what exactly just happened. This is the beginning of what will become a ***healing journey***.

and

2) As part of the re-grouping process, come to terms with the what/when/where/how of the emotional accident so that as they move forward again they are prepared for what is to come. For example, on a metaphorical level, are there more "screeching cars out of control in the

I Didn't Mean For This To Happen

distance" and should they prepare for further emotional blindsiding or car accident scenes? Perhaps it is the road they are on that is causing all these cars to spin out of control and they need to abandon travel plans all together and get to higher ground for safety? Or was this scene containable to the acting-out party's one car and the crash is over? Hurting parties have to get a sense of what they are even dealing with as the crisis comes out of nowhere and is causing all kinds of wreckage.

Acting-out parties need to answer the question of the what/when/where/how variables of their acting-out.

For example:

What: What is the acting-out party doing exactly? What were they thinking while doing that?

Who: Who was the acting-out party involved with while acting-out? Who else knows?

When: When did all this happen? How long has this been going on?

Where: Where did all this acting-out happen? Who else knows about this?

How: How much acting-out has occurred and how long has the acting-out been going on?

Then hurting parties can make an informed decision around exactly what it is that they are even dealing with in terms of the acting-out. For instance, is the acting-out party totally out of control and for safety reasons does the hurting party need to pack up the children and run for safety? Is the acting-out of a criminal nature and does the hurting party need to explore issues as well as get professional support around the implications of the acting-out party offending? Was there child abuse with the acting-out and is there a possibility with sexual acting-out that this behaviour could escalate to child abuse? Does a secondary level of authorities (if this is a criminal matter) and professionals need to be involved in this situation because the problem is bigger than the two of you? If there has been sexual acting-out are the hurting parties at risk for sexually transmittable infections or HIV? Do they need to go and get medical tests from their Doctors because of possible exposure of their spouses having unprotected sex with others? If there has been financial overspending and acting-out, exactly how much debt has accumulated and will they be at risk for bankruptcy or collections issues with no way to pay for outstanding debts that have been accumulated?

Hurting parties cannot make informed decisions around what to do until they know the nature as well as facts of what it is exactly they are dealing with outside of the lies as well as stories from the acting-out parties. This is why it is so important for acting-out parties to be honest especially out of fairness to hurting parties. Also hurting parties really need to get a sense of whether there will be further emotional fall-out from the acting-out. For example, if an outside lover is involved in an affair does the acting-out party want to maintain contact further and continue the relationship? Is the mistress possibly pregnant and will be having a baby out of the affair? Is the acting-out party in love with the mistress and will he be leaving the marriage to start a long term relationship with that mistress? With a sense of knowing the who/what/when/where/how variables, hurting parties can determine if there is going to be further emotional damage or potential emotional blindsiding fall-out through more metaphorical car crashes to come or not.

A Deep Injury At An Emotional Level

What hurting parties signed up for in their marriages is not what they are getting and they are at the scene of a metaphorical

I Didn't Mean For This To Happen

car accident trying to make sense of the curled metal, the smoke and flames, and the wreckage that is lying before them. They have to make sense of the impact of the wreckage and determine how as well as why this occurred? For some hurting parties, they will need to just get out of the flames as well as smoke and go to higher ground for safety (leave the scene) and then regroup later. Once away from the scene, hurting parties can explore the nature of the accident scene and the likelihood of whether this will happen again. For example, will the acting-out party agree to go for counselling? Does the acting-out party recognize their behaviour is wrong? Are they willing to *own the wreckage* and do the necessary work to change so that this will not happen again? How does the acting-out party even make sense of all of this damage? What were they thinking? What do they want moving forward?

While getting the answers to these questions, hurting parties can then make a determination in their own minds around their commitment levels to the relationship by determining the chances or likelihood of the acting-out behaviour occurring again and what this emotional accident scene means to their lives? Also they must reconcile in time the image of who they married versus the reality of the acting-out behaviours before them. For example, many hurting parties wonder if the acting-out party could do this, then what else are they capable of doing? Or what else is not being said at this point? Essentially, how deep is the acting-out behaviour and is this something that surfaced only during the marriage or well before the relationship even started?

With disclosure, acting-out parties become honest about the deceptions of the past by answering the who/what/when/where/how questions. Acting-out parties decide whether they are going to do a *full disclosure* (admit everything in detail) or a *partial disclosure* (cover the necessary facts in terms of the overall theme, nature, or flavor of the acting-out behaviour). For example, if a husband with a sex addiction had 35 affairs outside of the marriage through his sexual acting-out he is not going to go into detail about each individual affair. He may also not be able to remember. Instead, this husband may resolve to do a partial disclosure and he can answer the critical questions of whether his wife is safe and needs to be tested for diseases along with the other who/what/when/where/how questions with generalities. Also, the wife will inevitably want to know not about each individual sexual acting-out episode but whether this acting-out was with people she knows and has friendships with so that she can prepare for any secondary emotional fall-out in her own circle of personal friendships or associations.

Hurting parties also want to be careful of the questions that they ask. At the time, hurting parties may think they really want to know all the intricate details of the acting-out behaviour, but they need to keep in mind that the description of these behaviours becomes part of visuals that will stick in the minds of the hurting parties. If they are not careful, these visuals will play over and over again in their minds as they try to work out these situations of broken trust. For some people, these visuals of the acting-out become "burned in their minds" several years after the fact and may be part of a "sticking point" that they just cannot get over.

For example, with the knowledge that a husband had sex in the family home with his mistress, the hurting party spouse may not be able to get over this level of deep betrayal because of the perceived blatant disregard for her feels deeply personal. The husband may have chosen the family home out of convenience and as part of his "high" in acting-out which added to the risk factor and made the sex that much more exciting. With that image in the wife's mind, she may struggle to recover from such wound-

I Didn't Mean For This To Happen

ing. Everyone reacts differently, and some wives have been able to rebound from this detail because the husband has made such a commitment to changing that the past does not have a complete hold on the relationship. Also the wife and husband may have sold the house or renovated the bedroom so that the "scene of the crime of the affair" is not so blatant.

Sticking with the facts and being careful as to the level of detail are important guidelines for hurting parties to follow. Remember this is "material that will play over and over again in your head" until you work it all out. Also, the level of healing the overall relationship or marriage will be contingent on the acting-out parties' level of honesty and the ability to understand the impact of their behaviours as they correct the wrong they have done. If acting-out parties continue to make excuses for their behaviours, are not honest, and are not accountable as well as responsible for their actions then reconciliation will be next to impossible. There will not be a new start and opportunity for major transformation. Instead, acting-out parties will continue doing what they do best which is acting-out and hurting parties can expect more of the same behaviours.

Acting-out parties are also in a *preoccupation* (focused on the anticipated high of the acting-out) as well as *ritualization* (the process of getting the high or acting-out) phases which is much like a trance whereby they lose all sense of time as well as direction because they are so focused on their acting-out behaviors. Yes, they are one hundred percent accountable for their actions but while acting-out so many times or also by burying the details into their subconscious out of shame, they may genuinely not remember every time they acted-out. In fact, such people might not be able to explain exactly what they were thinking at each important interval in the acting-out. Instead, these people were in a type of tunnel vision or trance by being so immersed in the conquest of acting-out that they lost touch with reality. For example, Geoff sexually acted-out with prostitutes and he was so immersed in the anticipation of acting-out that he forgot to pick up his kids from school on several occasions. Also, he cannot recall all the times he attended the bath houses or locations he went to with prostitutes. Instead, Geoff was completely immersed in his fantasy world and at times totally out of touch with reality.

Acting-out parties can explain their overall general thought process as to what they were thinking and the types of things that happened along the way, but they may not actually remember to the full extent that hurting parties may want them to. Also acting-out parties may not remember exact dates or times and their time-line may be vague. As a result of being in the *"me-bubble"* (selfish preoccupation), they have been so absorbed into their thinking that they have *compartmentalized* sections of their life and buried these details from conscious memory. In some ways, they may not "want to go there" in details and because of repressed shame they may not "be able to even allow themselves to remember to go there." Sometimes people who act-out actually remember more details after the fact especially if they are attending therapy and counselling. In their minds, these details through therapy may be "lesser offences" of the acting-out or just similar variations that came to mind. It is important for acting-out parties to not re-visit disclosure and have a "Oh by the way I forgot to tell you" moment with hurting parties or this process will be much like ripping the scab off of a wound on a metaphorical level. Disclosure is an upfront step that should not be re-visited once completed.

After disclosure is completed, then hurting parties can begin sharing the overall impact of the acting-out behaviours on them.

I Didn't Mean For This To Happen

The Process of Healing:
1) Acting-out party provides disclosure
2) Hurting party asks clarification questions around the disclosure
3) Hurting party discusses or shares impact of acting-out behaviour
4) Question of "what is going to be different?" must be answered for the couple to move on towards reconciliation in the future of their relationship.

Authentic Vagueness

The acting-out party is honest to their best ability but because of shame or being so immersed in the acting-out behaviour they cannot provide all the details of exactly all the times they acted-out. Instead, they can explain the overall nature of the acting-out and what they were thinking along with answering very important safety questions that will inevitably impact the hurting party. Then the hurting party can make an informed decision around how to make sense of the acting-out and what this means for their lives.

Planning Carefully For Disclosure

Acting-out parties must carefully consider disclosure and should plan such a disclosure with their therapist or mentor to review the details that they will disclose. If an individual is resigning themselves to a ***partial disclosure*** then they will need to make a commitment to partially disclosing and not shift from their position. For example, if a husband hired over fifty prostitutes then he may resign himself to disclosing that he had sex with multiple prostitutes without naming the number. The main point in the disclosure is that he must be prepared to answer questions of whether his wife will need to get tested for sexually transmittable diseases as well as be prepared to answer questions like what was he thinking, how could he do such a thing, and is his wife's safety at risk?

Disclosure is difficult but necessary because the emotionally-injured partner on the receiving end of the broken trust must be able to make an informed decision on whether they want to continue on the road to reconciliation in the marriage. Also, in fairness to both partners, couples need to really examine the extent of the lies and deceptions that are now compromising the safety as well as integrity of their marriages.

Some couples do not need disclosure because they are aware of the events. For example, some husbands who have a fantasy obsession with pornography have been up during the evenings when their wives' were asleep watching pornography and masturbating. Such behaviour was part of an irregular "peaks and valleys" experience that was intense during some times and not during other phases in the marriage. The wife does not have a safety concern and there was no physical infidelity. Therefore the healing is more contingent upon the husband's ability to understand the impact of his behaviours rather than exploring the nature of the lies and deceptions. In fact, he watched pornography and that was the extent of his lies.

The amount of energy that people put into disclosure depends on individual circumstances. One critical point, however, is that once disclosure has occurred the acting-out party will be asked if that is all there is to disclose? Trust in relationships and the reconciliation process cannot move forward if the person who broke trust keeps revisiting the disclosure issue. For example, a husband says later "oh by the way there was another situation that I didn't mention because I did not want to hurt you." Couples cannot keep revisiting the disclosure issue because safety in the relationship will not be established. In the disclosure phase, the

I Didn't Mean For This To Happen

partner who broke the trust must carefully consider what they are disclosing because the future of the relationship hinges on the safety and openness of the disclosure phase. Revisiting disclosure again down the line is like re-opening a wound and the process is torturous for partners who are already suffering from the injury of broken trust. The challenge for partners who have broken trust is to rise to a more mature level and "own" as well as be accountable for their past behaviours and the *wreckage* they have created.

Door Hinge #1 (Step Two) Validating The Injured Partner's Experience:

An important part of attending to the emotional wreckage is for partners who have broken trust to honour as well as validate the experiences of their spouses who were on the receiving end of the lies and deceptions. Trust cannot be rebuilt unless partners who broke trust are **accountable for the wreckage** they have created. In this stage, injured partners share their pain and experience of the past behaviours. Acting-out parties who have broken trust must be open to understanding the nature of the impact of their actions. This step may be done in couple's counselling or in the privacy of a couple's relationship. Some injured partners will write out their feelings and experiences. This process is part of cleaning a slate and beginning a stage of healing. The challenge for acting-out parties is to rise to higher maturity levels and really hear as well as validate the wreckage they have created.

This step will not be successful if the person who broke trust acts defensive and justifies their behaviours. For example an acting-out partner may say: "Why are we focusing on just me because you weren't exactly an angel in this marriage either!" This step is not an emotional mud-slinging scene. The point in healing is to own and attend to the wreckage that was created. In couple's therapy at a later time, couples may wish to explore resentments on each side of the marriage. This is not the time or place to compare each other's emotional dirty laundry. Individuals who have broken trust will be challenged to remain calm, empathic, and to listen during this process. Again, this step is like metaphorically attending to the emotional wound in the marriage.

The Impact Letter

Hurting parties may also feel empowered as they share their "voice" by talking about the impact of the acting-out behaviours. Some hurting parties will talk about the impact through a letter that they read to the acting-out parties.

Some considerations for the letter include:

1) The letter is a way of putting containment to the emotional injury and describing with words the impact of the acting-out behaviours.

2) With an impact letter, acting-out parties can better understand the impact of their behaviours and see that such actions were not harmless. Such a process helps to challenge the *fog of unhealthy thinking*, so that acting-out parties can no longer delude themselves into thinking that there is no emotional fall-out if they decide to *play in the shadows of life*.

3) With an impact letter, people can provide closure on the issue or have a sense that this issue was attended to as well as resolved.

4) With an impact letter, there is enhanced good-will in the relationship because the acting-out party is showing that they are taking responsibility for their behaviours by listening to the impact on the hurting party.

5) Acting-out parties can claim responsibility for their behaviours and as a result now start walking a path of

I Didn't Mean For This To Happen

accountability as they make the commitment towards positive change.

6) Both parties can re-set the relationship and start over while negotiating new roles as they talk about how things in their relationship will be **different** in the future.

7) Both parties can determine a sense of *that was then* and *this is now* while discussing how things will be better.

8) Hurting parties can receive validation and begin cleaning the wound as well as healing from the emotional injury.

9) Hurting parties can put closure on the issue while then moving on to managing their fears through their own independent work in their healing journeys or through counselling.

10) Acting-out parties can see where "things went wrong" and how they descended into their *fog of unhealthy thinking* while *playing in the shadows of life*. As a result, the snare or trap of acting-out is clear when they realize the impact of their behaviours on others.

When hurting parties share their impact letters with acting-out parties, it is important for the acting-out parties who broke the trust to lower their defenses, really listen, and create a safe emotional place to hear the impact of their actions. This way, actual healing can take place.

Door Hinge #2 (Step Three) Putting Safeguards In Place:
During this step the couple will explore *how things are going to be different* so that the *emotional wreckage* and the broken trust does not occur again in the marriage. During this process if affairs were involved, individuals must agree not to maintain

contact with their lovers and so on. Other people may need to remove the computer which was a vehicle for pornography or put other safeguards in place like computer censor software programs like "Covenant Eyes" and so on. Also individuals who have broken trust will need to work through their healing by putting accountabilities in place such as an *accountability partner, accountability systems*, and *accountability communities* which we will explore in the next chapter. Acting-out parties may also want to consider therapy with a counsellor or Psychologist to identify and put into place skills that will help them change their cycles of lying and acting-out. For some people this will involve a journey towards maintaining sexual purity as well as ending the cycle of lying. These safeguards are necessary for trust to be re-established in relationships once again. Another option around accountabilities and growing from this crisis of broken trust is to participate in the Real Life Tool Box on-line programs and courses around healing and recovery (www.reallifetoolbox.com).

Door Hinge #3 (Step Four) Maintaining Rigorous Honesty:
The hurt that partners feel from broken trust does not automatically go away and does begin to heal over time once spouses start *working a program*. An accountability or recovery program involves changing all the old thinking patterns and actions related to their lying, deceits, as well as acting-out behaviors. Over time hurting parties can then develop the assurance to lower their guards and become emotionally-invested in the future of their relationships. The couple can transform out of this "crash and burn experience" and grow closer as well as stronger together. The key ingredient to moving forward is creating and sustaining honesty in the relationship.

If partners who have broken trust begin lying again (even about the smallest details) then there will be a tsunami effect in their relationships. For example, the newfound pain from the new lies will match the pain from the past lies and their partners will experience a tsunami of hurt emotion from the compounded pain over time. Also, if acting-out partners do not start to own their feelings, communicate, and end the lying cycle then they themselves are placing themselves in a vulnerable predicament in which they can easily kick-start the chain of acting-out behaviours again. All lies, addictions, and broken trust behaviours start with individuals lying to themselves, becoming defensive, and then slowly sliding down the slippery slope back into the old behaviours. Honesty is the flashlight in the shadows of life and acting-out behaviours thrive in the darkness as well as shadows. Therefore **rigorous honesty** is absolutely essential in the healing and sustainability of marriages with broken trust issues.

When Trust is Never Healed

The above four steps are critical for the rebuilding process and serve as the doorway to the road to reconciliation. The following situations are traps that people can fall into so that they end up compromising the trust rebuilding process. While working through these four steps, people need to be mindful of potential emotional pitfalls.

Pitfall #1: Revisiting disclosure

Relationships will not heal without safety. Safety cannot be created if individuals keep revisiting the disclosure issue and one partner changes or repeatedly lies about the details of their earlier transgressions or dishonourable actions.

Pitfall #2: The Acting-Out Party is defensive

Relationships cannot heal if the partner who broke the trust continues to make excuses for their behaviours. For example a partner says: "Well I have great sexual needs so of course I need pornography. You can never satisfy me in that way."

Pitfall #3: The Acting-Out Party refuses to change

Relationships cannot heal if the partner who broke trust refuses to change their behaviours or they keep using excuses. For example, individuals may leave open "loopholes" or "backdoors" as a way to secure opportunities to return to their old behaviours. For example, a husband who had an affair with his boss says that he will not change his job or department at work and that his wife will just have to trust him next time.

Pitfall #4: There is no recovery or healing program in place

When people begin this healing process they need to put supports in place and follow not only an ***accountability and recovery program*** but also introduce healthy habits into their lives. Acting-out parties must have ***accountability partners***, ***accountability systems***, and ***accountability communities***. Also acting-out parties may want to participate in the Real Life Tool Box on-line programs and courses such as "Finding Freedom" so that they gain a toolbox filled with skills for how to manage the fog of unhealthy thinking so that they do not play in the shadows of life with their unhealthy acting-out behaviours. Individual should not just assume that they can heal their acting-out behaviours themselves without supports because they cannot develop the necessary objectivity to manage the *fog of unhealthy thinking* that can descend within their own minds. Most people need therapy and a an *accountability and recovery program* that they can use to stay on track towards maintaining positive change.

Pitfall #5: The Hurting Party is haunted by images from the disclosure

Spouses of broken trust can benefit from receiving therapy themselves as they begin their own healing journeys. Often hurting parties will have images in their minds of the lies, affairs, or acting-out behaviours that they feel haunted by as they experience

I Didn't Mean For This To Happen

a type of emotional flashback. With help and support they can work through these feelings and experiences as well as liberate themselves from the cycle of rage, hopelessness, self-doubt, insecurities, and self-loathing that can come from experiencing broken trust in their marriages.

Will We Make It?

Marriages do survive infidelity, addiction, pornography /fantasy obsessions, or other forms of broken trust all the time. Such a process is like being in a rowboat whereby the couple establishes a direction and shared vision of the future. In the healing, couples resolve their emotional issues and become even stronger as a result of their experiences. Individuals must, however, follow the four steps above with great care, dedication, as well as commitment because if one partner does not commit to working on this process they are on a metaphorical level tossing their oars out of the rowboat and the momentum as well as course set for the future becomes compromised. At that point, couples may want to on a figurative level row in their own boats for a while as they work through their healing or recovery journeys. The success of this process works if both partners are committed to the steps and take turns *working in the solution* by eagerly taking up the oars when it is their turn to work these stages of healing. Both sides must be dedicated to the overall healing of the marriage on all emotional levels and there must be a great degree of safety, honesty, as well as accountability to fuel this process.

Chapter 4
How Do We Move Forward?

If people want to free themselves from the patterns of the past and the old acting-out behaviours as well as cycles of broken trust, then they must be prepared to make the shift from *playing in the shadows of life* to *living in the light*. This means that we live with accountability as well as responsibility around all of our actions in life. Such a transition is one from emotional immaturity to full scale emotional as well as spiritual maturity. There are no excuses and we step into who God has called us to be in this world so that we can carry out His larger calling or purpose for our lives.

In order to live in the light, we must actively do "gatekeeping" to keep the shadows of life at a distance and to *manage the fog of unhealthy thinking*. This is a conscious as well as intentional choice so that we actually *work* our healing and/or recovery with a program around having *accountability partners, accountability systems*, and *accountability communities*. We have to be prepared to answer the question of **what will be different** in our lives?

When Red Flags Turn Green

When people are in the *fog* of acting-out, they misinterpret warning signs. Such individual are in a type of *tunnel vision* with *emotional blinders* on and they are so preoccupied with their CER (*controlled emotional release*) or "perceived feel good" that nothing else matters at that moment. These people have lost touch with the larger picture issues and are not considering the emotional wreckage they are creating for themselves. Then when the consequences hit and their spouses and families are mad at them, they have spent money they should not have, or there is some type of emotional fall-out or wreckage, then such people feel shame for their behaviours. When they were in the midst of the acting-out, however, they were in *tunnel vision*.

We know we are dealing with addictions when bad things are happening as a result of the acting-out and we continue anyways. In essence, we are turning "red flags" into "green ones" while ignoring danger signals in our own lives. We stay in tunnel vision and continue on in the acting-out without considering the ramifications.

Can you stick to a limit with your acting-out behaviour or do you bargain with the behaviour and always exceed your limit?

For example:

-I will only drink one glass of wine and then I drink an entire bottle.

-I will only spend fifty dollars gambling and then I have racked up my credit card.

-I will only look at one quick site on the internet, and then several hours passes by as I masturbate to pornography.

-I agree I will only play my on-line game for one round and an entire evening passes by.

What Is An Accountability Partner?

A person or selected individuals who *call out red flags* in your life around your habit. Such people help you to manage your unhealthy thinking. When you are in the fog of unhealthy thinking, your accountability partner helps you to identify that "fog." You can check in with your accountability partner regularly to discuss your progress and how you are doing.

What Is An Accountability System?

I Didn't Mean For This To Happen

The accountability system is the *brakes* in your life and the elimination of opportunities to "act-out." For example, a person with a sex addiction may put computer monitoring software on their computer, place their computer in an open space in the house, and so forth. What accountabilities can you put into place so that you are eliminating or at the very least making it very difficult for yourself to "act-out?"

Stepping From The Shadows Into The Light

In the shadows of life, we can pull out two large double-size flash lights called *responsibility* and *accountability* in order to navigate through the darkness of our lives. Ultimately, the largest flood light is God and in the next chapter we will examine how to bring the Lord back into the center of your life. But for now as we work a path of healing and/or recovery, we must manage the shadows that are in our worlds.

What is responsibility?

Responsibility: being answerable for the actions as well as decisions that are within your control.

With responsibility, we say: "yes this is a problem and we want to do something about it!" We actively stop the cycles of blaming or using excuses and we have answers for the good and bad choices we make in life. Essentially, we *own* our behaviours and make decisions to do what is right.

What is accountability?

Accountability: explaining or reporting about the actions that are within your control.

With accountability, we do what is right, good, and virtuous. This is not a starvation diet or a life of sacrifice. We can acknowledge the self-destructive nature of unhealthy behaviours and stop fooling ourselves. The acting-out behaviour is a "poison" in life and it negatively affects relationships as well as overall qualities of life. When we are in the "thick of it", we do not see how we are harming ourselves or impacting others around us. With accountability, we steer the course of doing what is right and good while reporting back about our progress.

Why We Should Put Accountabilities In Place:

#1 Reason: We lie to ourselves and begin to have the *fog of unhealthy thinking* descend into our thoughts. In fact, we can justify or make anything okay to ourselves by deceiving ourselves into believing that:

a) we can handle the CER

b) that the CER is not hurting anyone

c) we will do the CER "just this one time."

As a result of this unhealthy thinking:

- we have spent money we shouldn't have

- we have put others at risk

- we have lied and manipulated in order to make accommodations for the CER and escape life.

-we do not like who we have become in the compulsion or addiction and want to make positive changes.

-we have lost much personal freedom in our bondage as well as enslavement to the CER and escape life. The CER is always on our minds and we do not feel free.

-we are not who we want to be in God's design for our lives.

-we are not having fun anymore with the acting-out behaviours.

-we are starting to lose everything.

-our partners are having to "mop up emotional messes" and are exhausted/burned-out from chasing down the truth because of all of the lies.

-we don't want to be doing this and in this same place 10 years from now.

I Didn't Mean For This To Happen

The Self-Pride Block

As an acting-put party, you may find an initial resistance to having accountabilities in place because you want to "be normal" and "just like everyone else." In some ways, you may even feel like a child who is in trouble and this is your grounding. Also you may feel shameful like you are admitting failure, defeat, or that there is something wrong with you.

The reality is that you are not a failure. Many people have an unhealthy attachment to a CER whether it be eating, spending money, acting-out with sex, and so forth. With accountabilities, you are shining the spotlight on the shadows of your life. Sin, lies, deceits, manipulations, and so forth thrive in the shadows of secrecy in this world. There is tremendous courage involved in bringing these shadows out into the open and into the light of God's healing. When we step into the light and have accountabilities in place to keep us in that light, then we can gain freedom. We no longer have to live in the ensnarement of sin. In Mathew 5:29 we are called to remove anything that causes us to "stumble."

Healthiness Is A Constant Choice

The point is to not go through this process and just decide that you want to be strong in your mind and just stop. When we are powered by self-will, we are vulnerable to the ***fog of unhealthy thinking*** descending into our thoughts. We will start lying to ourselves and we bargain with the acting-out, compulsion, or addiction. Suddenly we will make it okay to use our CER just a little bit.

Recovery is about staying on top of your thinking. My saying is:

"Remember you must stay on top of your thinking, or your thinking will stay on top of you!"

Cathy Patterson-Sterling

Healthiness and wellness is a conscious choice. It is the 250 decisions we make each day. For example at a point in the day should we go for the cookie or the banana? Healthy people are healthy by conscious choice and with work. You do not wake up declared healthy. We are the sum of all of our choices. The beer belly is instant proof of that!

Working Recovery And Healing As Part Of A Journey

In order to manage the *fog of unhealthy thinking* and to work your recovery and/or healing journey you will need an *accountability partner* along the way. An accountability partner is a person who coaches another person in terms of keeping a commitment. The concept of an accountability partner was originally used for weight loss in the 1960's. People would set their weight loss goals and an accountability partner was someone who they could check-in with and talk about whether they were meeting their goals or not. The term accountability partner is now even used for people who are setting up small businesses and want to meet their goals for staying on track with their vision for their business.

What Is A CPA?

A CPA is a *commitment of positive action*. In the recovery or healing journey, people are making commitments towards positive action so they are called CPA's.

CPA's have sorted out in their minds the line between being healthy and "crossing the line" towards being unhealthy. This is a major positive action and the promise they are making is positive for their lives as well as for others around them. For example, a person may make a commitment of positive action by no longer drinking alcohol.

Therefore there is an **accountability partner** and their **CPA** (commitment of positive action) person. A CPA has made a commitment of positive action to be healthy and not cross a line or limit that they have set as part of their healing or recovery.

Examples of Common CPA Lines (line of healthiness or sobriety):
-not drinking alcohol
-not acting-out sexually
-not engaging in on-line gaming
-not gambling
-following proper food limits and not emotional eating
-not engaging in compulsive shopping or overspending of money
-maintaining monogamy and healthy levels of emotional availability in a relationship
-not lusting
-not having inappropriate dialogue with others over the internet
-not flirting or being overly "familiar" with others which could lead to emotional affairs
-not going outside of the marriage to meet sexual needs
-not over-working or engaging in compulsive levels of working
-not viewing pornography
-not trying to control or obsess about someone else's unhealthy behaviours

What Are Good Qualities Of An Accountability Partner?

1) Listens well
   James 1:19
   My dear brothers and sisters, take note of this: Everyone should be quick to listen, slow to speak and slow to become angry,

2) Caring
   1John 4:21
   And he has given us this command: Anyone who loves God must also love their brother and sister.

3) Is well-grounded and is inspiring
   Accountability partners should be healthy on an emotional level and have something to offer in terms of inspiring that same level of health or level of spiritual maturity in others.
4) Same gender
   Accountability partners and their CPA's should be the same gender. This way relationships do not become complicated and there is not any potential for emotional affairs or jealousies with people's spouses.
5) Genuine
   Accountability partners should be genuine as well as authentic in that they are "real" and are able to walk beside others in a real and non-superficial way.
6) Offers support
   Accountability partners give of themselves and are able to offer well-needed support to their CPA.
7) Available
   Accountability partners need to be able to be accessible to their CPA (s) by phone, in person, via e-mail or all of the above.
8) Regular schedule
   Accountability partners and their CPA (s) should have a regular schedule for meeting in person or through phone-calls to check-in.
9) May be part of a team
   A CPA may have more than one accountability partner and as such might have an accountability team. Each accountability partner needs to have regular scheduled time with the CPA.
10) Able to confront in a caring way

I Didn't Mean For This To Happen

An accountability partner needs to be able to confront in a caring way and help the CPA if they are veering away from or making excuses not to engage in the commitment of positive action.

Accountability partners help CPA's stay focused as well as keep on track with the commitment of positive action. In fact by meeting regularly, accountability partners help CPA's "stay in the healthy conversation" by keeping the commitment of positive action at the forefront of lives. CPA's do not allow busyness to take over their worlds which results in the diminishing of the commitment of positive action. When accountability partners and CPA's meet regularly they add new energy as well as renewed and ongoing commitment towards the positive action that has been promised originally by these CPA's.

Accountability partners serve a critical purpose as they offer support and a second opinion or they assist CPA's by looking at situations from different angles. Also accountability partners help CPA's celebrate victories along the way of the healing and/or recovery journey.

Managing The Fog

In a healing or recovery journey people are attached to unhealthy behaviours because such old ways of thinking or acting have become very familiar. Therefore when individuals encounter challenges they will often go back to the old ways which is much like a "default" setting or "automatic pilot" (a return to the same ways they have always done things.) New healthy habits involve conscious intent to want to do things differently and this often requires venturing into the unknown. Rather than approaching situations in a healthy manner without knowing the instant results, people will often gravitate back to old ways of coping. Such old ways are the *fog of unhealthy thinking*. A large part of an accountability partner's role is to notice when the CPA is "getting foggy" in their thinking or making excuses for why they cannot follow through with their commitment of positive action. Accountability partners will "point out the fog" and help them to clear their thinking by looking at situations from multiple angles while being challenged to use healthy ways of responding.

Your Accountability System

CPA's need to look at their emotional triggers towards unhealthiness. What are the people/places/things/ways of thinking/situations that draw them away from being strong in their commitment of positive action? Then CPA's need to create a system for how they will manage these negative influences.

For example:

The person who struggles with alcohol needs to remove all alcohol from their home and make sure they do not put themselves in high risk situations whereby they will be more prone to drink. Also the individual needs to sort through what unhelpful thinking patterns they have or triggers that may result in cravings to drink alcohol. For example, will they need to manage boredom, self-pity, or other negative patterns of thinking?

A person who struggles with pornography will need to either remove access to the computer or put on computer filters and screening software programs like "Covenant Eyes" or "Net Nanny" etc. With the Covenant Eyes software program the accountability partner may receive a copy of reports listing the websites the CPA has visited and as part of the accountabilities the accountability partner may organize with the CPA to report to a third party like the CPA's spouse any inappropriate sites that have been visited.

Your Accountability Community

An accountability community may be a group of CPA's who meet together, a church group, a bible study, or a recovery group.

I Didn't Mean For This To Happen

CPA's need to manage the fog of unhealthy thinking and "get out of their heads." CPA's can renew their commitment of positive action by getting out regularly and talking with people so that they can look at their situations from multiple angles and not get trapped into old thinking patterns or ways of dealing with things.

An accountability community may also be virtual. Real Life Toolbox has groups called POD Tutorials whereby CPA's may find 10 or more peers with similar issues who want to meet in an on-line tutorial with an on-line wellness coach to have a meeting to discuss healing journey or recovery journey related issues. With Real Life Toolbox, there are accountability partner training programs, recovery and healing journey courses, healing and recovery journey plans with an on-line wellness coach, as well as all kinds of life skills programs. Check out www.reallifetoolbox.com for more details.

Some Key Points About Community:

-As people we are healthiest in community.

-In recovery and healing, we need to "get out of our heads" and into life.

-There is tremendous power in fellowship. God wants us to be in His community.

The Healing Journey For Hurting Parties

Just like how acting-out parties have their own recovery/healing journeys, so do hurting parties have their own healing journeys. Hurting parties are challenged to move through the layers of feelings they experience around the crisis of broken trust. Also once the acting-out behaviour is contained, hurting parties may discover that there is much emotional wreckage or even damage within themselves as a result of their patterns of trying to manage the unhealthiness of others. Therefore while on a healing journey, hurting parties have an opportunity to reclaim back their lives as they as move through the tunnel of feelings, get themselves back by working on enhancing their emotional core, enhance their self-care or self-esteems, learn about boundaries as well as limits, and grow in their confidence as well as personal value. The result is that hurting parties can then turn all of this pain as well as upset into fuel for personal transformation. As a result, they become better people and with their partners working the recovery steps they will have stronger marriages. An important starting point may be to not only read this book but also read another book I have written called *Core Confidence: Stepping Into Your Greatest Potential-Stepping Into Your Greatest Life* while also visiting www.real-lifetoolbox.com to explore the different on-line programs, courses, and POD tutorials for hurting parties on their journeys to healing. Also hurting parties may want to work through a *personal care plan* with their own on-line wellness coach while also attending virtual POD tutorials with others Christians who are on a similar journey to healing from the impact of broken trust in their lives.

Chapter 5
Releasing Ourselves From The Shadow Of The Past

The crisis of broken trust is a powerful time in life because there is so much pain. We are forced to dig deep to the core of who we are and really look within the shadows of ourselves. Furthermore, we have an option then of stepping into God's light as we transform from these experiences and grow into the potential of who God designed us to be so that we can carry out His higher purpose in life. Such a process of transformation requires the accountability as well as responsibility of shining the light into the shadows while also keeping the *fog of unhealthy thinking* free from ourselves by *working* a healing or recovery journey. As we start building accountabilities into place so that we are no longer participating in self-destructive acting-out behaviours, we are challenged to grow on deeper emotional as well as spiritual levels. We can no longer hide from ourselves with the CER (*controlled emotional release*) of sexually acting-out, pornography, lusting, compulsive spending, on-line gaming, emotional eating, gambling, and so on. Instead, we have the option of looking at the deeper broken or wounded parts of ourselves that need to be healed. This may require that we die unto old parts of ourselves like with self-pride, inflated ego, insecurities, and so forth as we let go of the emotional crutch of the CER to begin growing into our potential as people. This is a scary but exciting time in life because where we are going is completely unknown and this is the step of faith that the Lord will guide us at each moment towards His larger will.

Hurting parties also have the opportunity for incredible transformation through the crisis of broken trust because with their tremendous level of pain, they are required to dig deep and identify the old parts of themselves which they need to die unto as well. Likely hurting parties may even have a sense of "losing themselves" as they became drawn into the ***chaos vortex*** of trying to manage the unhealthy behaviours of the acting-out parties in their lives. Therefore hurting parties can through their healing journey begin a process of "getting themselves back", learning about boundaries, finding their emotional cores, enhancing confidence, ending cycles of people-pleasing, and so forth as they grow into their greatest potential in God's larger design for their lives.

Where We Are Going

The past no longer has a "hold" on us when we are more excited about where we are going than where we have been in life. This is much like being in a power boat and our focus can be behind us in the wake and the wash or we can look through the windshield at the front of us. In order to focus forward, we need something inspiring to look at as we concentrate on moving forward. Our attention is not on where we have been, but where we are going. In fact, the crisis of broken trust can become a positive defining moment of transformation whereby acting-out parties as well as hurting parties decide to attend to the deeper unresolved emotional issues in their lives that have always been there but have been ignored for a long time. Rather than escaping into busyness, people can do some deeper learning as well as growing around who they are, their motivations in life, unhelpful coping behaviours and CER's, as well as get clear about what they want in this world.

I Didn't Mean For This To Happen

The bottom line of any positive change in relationships is the ability to answer the question *"**What is going to be different?**"* In order for couples to move beyond the past, they must be able to answer this question of what will be different in their lives or they will be drawn back into the past. With responsibilities as well as accountabilities in place along with a commitment to recovery/healing journeys for acting-out parties and healing journeys for hurting parties, a brighter future is possible. People must have supports in place and they need to be *working* the healing involved because they cannot just "flick a switch" and "wipe the slate clean" by pretending the past did not occur. We can try to move forward as if nothing happened, but in the back of our minds we will live in fear worrying that the past will replay again in the future.

The Hope Meter

We will allow ourselves to look towards the future and free ourselves from the past when we have hope that there can be a brighter future. Such hope comes when we are doing what we are supposed to be doing in terms of having the responsibilities as well accountabilities in place while working our healing journeys. When we make a *commitment to positive action* (CPA) by drawing a new line of healthiness, and we keep doing what is necessary to maintain that promise then we do not have to be on guard with each other. Instead, we can trust that we are each doing what we need to do to make this relationship better. Also, when we do have emotional tangles the new skills that we are using will appear in that we will be more patient and take the time to work through difficult conversations even though there are challenges. By challenging ourselves to "hang in the hard places" of our relationships and by taking the time to listen as well as work through issues, we are *building good will*. With this good will over time we know that our partners are doing what they need to do to be healthy and that we are growing on deeper emotional as well as spiritual levels as well. When there is enough good will, we can allow ourselves to hope for a brighter future. Essentially, the hope meter in relationships increases and we can rebuild from the broken trust. As we become more excited about the future, the past no longer has such holds on us because we no longer feel like we are the people we were then. We have put an emotional distance between ourselves now and the past because we have grown as individuals as we focus on the future.

The North Star

When we do things differently and attend to the emotional issues of our lives then we can focus on a brighter future. Essentially, we can look at where we are going in life and not necessarily concentrate on where we have been because the past no longer has holds on us. The crisis of broken trust is an ugly moment in life, but it is not our life! When we build good will as well as hope back into the relationship through working our responsibilities as well as accountabilities along the healing journey, then we can allow ourselves to look at future goals or a "north star." The north star is the "why" of change and who we want to be in our futures. Our north stars individually as well as a couple may include a "bucket list" of things we want to be able to do before we pass away in this life. Much like the Jack Nicholson movie *The Bucket List* what do you want to do before you "kick the bucket" or pass away? When we have future goals of what we want to do we become emotionally-invested in the present as we look forward to where we are going in our relationships rather than reliving the past. With our north stars in mind (our future goals) we gain direction in life. When the emotional storms blow in and there are problems, we can reorient ourselves by moving through these is-

I Didn't Mean For This To Happen

sues through focusing on our "sight lines" or "north stars" of where we are going. We stop "going down in the small stuff" or "tripping" because we are able to "keep our eyes on the larger prize" of our north stars. In fact, we do not lose perspective because as a couple we know where we are going in life.

Managing The Haunting

Now hurting parties may have emotional flashbacks of pain whereby there are images in their minds of the broken trust or the feelings of profound emotional abandonment that they have experienced. For example, Robert wants to get excited about the future with his wife Lidia, however, he continues to remember how Lidia slept with his friend and he has images of them making love in his mind which brings him intense pain. Robert is "haunted" by the past. Now if Lidia is "working" her recovery/healing journey and doing all that she can with her *accountabilities* as well as *responsibilities* then she is growing on deeper emotional as well as spiritual levels. Lidia is no longer the insecure person she was who needed to get attention from Robert's friend because she was convinced that with all of Robert's long hours of work that he did not care about her. Lidia and Robert have concentrated on creating a new future and Lidia has answered the question of what will be different? She has attended counselling, actively connects with her accountability partners, attends on-line POD tutorial recovery meetings with her accountability community, and so on. Lidia is also attending school and is focused on all kinds of personal goals. She is no longer that insecure woman who was waiting in the wings of Robert's life. Lidia realized that Robert could not "fill the holes up in her heart" so she started doing the work of getting her own self-worth, core confidence, as well as self-esteem back.

Also Lidia and Robert talk all the time and have worked through their communication issues. Essentially, Lidia is not the same person she was before and their relationship has changed. Next Summer they are going to Italy and they are both excited to be learning a new language. Also both Lidia and Robert are doing daily devotionals together and actively praying as a couple as they take the time to check-in with each other. Lidia is regretful of the past and is completely repentant, but also Lidia and Robert are in a "good place" emotionally in their relationship. Lidia no longer flirts with other men and she makes sure Robert knows how much he is loved by her. In Robert's journey, he had to work through his feelings of hurt as well as fear. An important step along the way was *managing the haunting* of the past images of Lidia with another man. But as Robert gets excited about his future with Lidia and he admires who she has become, the past now serves as a memory that no longer has a hold over the two of them. Essentially, both Robert and Lidia have moved on into a brighter future as they grow into their larger potential of who they are meant to be in this world.

Chapter 6
The Potential Of Your Relationship

Shelley sat down with her hands firmly planted on the black leather couch of the therapist's office. She stared at the frames on the wall which included the licenses as well as degrees of the helping professional that she was about to meet within minutes. Shelley's husband entered the office and sat quietly on the opposite couch. He had a pensive expression as he greeted her in the voice of a whisper. This is not what Shelley had envisioned for her marriage and inside she felt like a failure.

When marriages are impacted by broken trust, spouses can feel like their relationships have become failures because they never anticipated that they would ever have such problems. Individuals often believe that difficulties are for other people and they never imagine that they will endure similar struggles. In such situations a deep level of faith is often needed because what may initially appear as pain as well as heartache can actually be used for good by God. The Lord takes us closer towards deeper spiritual transformation so we can then benefit from these experiences while moving closer to the larger design He has for our lives. With our free will and the free will of others troubling situations or problems do arise out of individuals' actions, but God does not waste a crisis and He can make immense good out of the bad in our worlds. Essentially, our pain is not in vain.

In marriages where trust is broken, people can live with regrets that they did not do certain things or that events unfolded in certain ways that now result in emotional upset for everyone involved. With deeper faith, we as Christians can realize that there are rarely accidents in life. Instead, God is always with us as He walks alongside in a personal relationship based on love. Yet, in relationships of broken trust people can feel like both their partners who were deceptive as well as God have abandoned them in a time of tremendous emotional pain. In fact, hurting parties who are on the receiving end of broken trust may feel like their partners have switched teams and gave up support because they were more focused on lying or acting in deceptive ways. Also these same hurting spouses who begin to heal may feel even more heartache as they come to terms with the details related to the broken trust behaviours. The initial part of healing can seem so painful that heartbroken spouses may feel like they are lost and as they pray for God to take the hurt away, the feelings of upset become that much more intense. As a result, such people believe that God is not answering their prayers for healing from their broken hearts.

In the early stages of healing, heartbroken spouses can feel a sense of complete hopelessness as if the life they knew and a sense of predictability has all but disappeared from their lives. On many levels, a spiritual hurricane has occurred as it swept through their emotional worlds and knocked down the security they had built in their marriages. The structures of the marriages they have created have been blown apart as these devastated spouses now examine the core or foundations of their marriages as they wonder whether it is really worth all the effort to rebuild again? Betrayed spouses have to search deep within their souls as they stare at

I Didn't Mean For This To Happen

the foundations of their relationships, wondering whether there is enough love left to rebuild their marriages.

A Time For Re-examination

With pain as well as struggles in marriages, people have to search deep within their core selves to sort through the strength involved in transforming from the pain. After trust is broken, there is a time of deep as well as honest self-examination. Betrayed spouses not only have a recoil effect of wondering what has happened to themselves and the lives they had planned for their families, but they also must do some critical soul work in order to transform in a positive way from such experiences. A crisis has occurred within these marriages and as a result couples with broken trust have to get clear about who they are, what they want out of life, and where to go from here. Such a thorough self-examination involves a look at couple's *interior* as well as *exterior* worlds. There is no doubt that people put a lot of energy into building up their "exterior" or outside worlds as they work hard to obtain their careers, homes, material assets, and so on as they make their environments comfortable. For many individuals of broken trust, however, the motivation to move forward to overcome personal challenges involves a great examination of their interior worlds which includes thoughts, values, personalities, motivations, and ways of being in their relationships.

The benefit of pain as well as crisis is that all extraneous details or irrelevant issues drop to the wayside. In crisis, people realize what is truly important in life and as they grow on deeper spiritual levels they can solidify their existing relationships with God. Such actions involve a testing of faith as people have to trust that God is indeed moving through their lives and that the decimation of their emotional houses in marriage is part of larger plans to rebuild their spiritual houses or relationships with God. Even in this time of extreme confusion, individuals can trust that God is indeed at the helm and is helping to guide this painful time for a larger purpose. God is good and we know from Jeremiah 29:11 that God has plans to prosper us.

Sometimes in life we can pick up ways of doing things that are not very helpful and our ideas as well as attitudes may become stuck so that as a result we stop growing emotionally. During crisis, God joins alongside us so that we can be released from these old ways of being and thinking as we grow into who we are really meant to be in this world. In fact, God has a larger design for our lives and pain as well as heartache is the fastest way to get our attention so that we change our ways of thinking and learn to approach life in a different way. This does not mean that we are not already faithful servants of God. We have to trust that even through there is crisis in our lives, there is also a larger plan and as servants of God we can believe that out of adversity will come blessings. God is walking alongside of us even if it does not appear that He is immediately answering our prayers to take the pain away from our lives.

Pioneering New Parts Of Ourselves

When trust is broken in marriages, many betrayed spouses pray that their partners will change and realize the errors of their ways. Broken trust and heartache is not just about people repenting their sins and is instead part of a larger, life-transforming experience. As people we operate out of unspoken rules, values, and ways of doing things from our families of origin. Sometimes our attitudes, thoughts, and beliefs are no longer working in our lives. For example the struggles we are having are not necessary if we grow as well as change so that we can rise to the occasion of what life demands out of us. For example, Victoria is devastated that

I Didn't Mean For This To Happen

she has found out her husband has a fantasy obsession with pornography and that he has been lying to her on countless occasions. As Victoria begins her journey of healing her husband's fantasy obsession becomes a catalyst for change in her own personal life. She does not realize that she struggles with fears of conflict and does not communicate her feelings to people because she worries that they will walk out her life. As a result, Victoria has *suffered in silence* with her husband's petulant behaviours.

Victoria's husband behaves like an emotional child who tantrums when he does not get his way. He is self-indulgent and focused on meeting his own needs. As a result, Victoria does all the work around their house as her husband behaves like an ungrateful child. He is not a spiritual leader of the household and is even more demanding than their own children. God walks alongside Victoria through the spiritual hurricane in their lives because He has great love for Victoria and her husband. In fact, this couple have a deeper calling to do mission work that they are not even aware of at this point because they are both stuck in emotional ruts. Now in crisis, both Victoria and her husband have the opportunity to grow on deeper emotional as well as spiritual levels. Victoria also does not realize that she is a gifted writer as well as speaker and through her journal writing of heartache around her husband's problems with pornography, she recognizes that she has a gift of expressing words. She is also an inspirational speaker who through this experience provides many other Christian women with an incredible sense of hope as well as renewed faith in their marriages. Victoria is courageous enough to use her personal testimony to inspire others. With her husband's problems, the result has been a positive chain reaction in a multitude of other people's lives.

Cathy Patterson-Sterling

There were many times that Victoria felt spiritually lost and believed that God had given up on her because of her intense pain as well as heartache. What she did not realize, however, was that together with her husband she had built a life based on image as well as impression management. She pretended to everyone else that everything in her life was fine. Victoria lived in a nice, upscale home but meanwhile her *interior world* was imploding as she disconnected from meaningful connections with her husband when he transgressed further into the world of pornography. Furthermore, Victoria could have pulled out the "unfair card of life" as she focused on how difficult her situation had become and that she did not deserve to have a husband who lied as well as manipulated others. Instead, she used her adversity as well as personal struggles as a way to grow on deeper emotional levels. By hitting an emotional bottom in life, Victoria grew from her adversity and soared to the heights in which God had intended for her world. God did not want Victoria to be a passive, wounded, fearful victim who was afraid of her own personal power as she pleased others in order to receive acceptance. Also God did not intend for her husband to be a demanding, self-centred child who acted like an emotional tyrant over his wife. Victoria's husband grew on deeper emotional as well as spiritual levels as a result of his recovery journey as well. He realized he did not have to be a scared little boy in life bullying others as a way to cope. Furthermore, he learned about his own potential and who he was meant to be as he connected with his deeper feelings, his value, and his goals in life.

Often there are times in life when the emotional systems we have in place as people will become train-wrecks or end up in problems later in life. In many ways, God with his mercy speeds up the already existing emotional train-wreck in motion and accelerates our worlds to a crisis point so that we can get the crisis

I Didn't Mean For This To Happen

over with faster and grow as well as transform on deeper levels. The blessing is that we connect with deeper meaning as well as purpose in our lives and also fulfill the larger design that God has for our lives.

Thus, people's unresolved emotional issues or baggage that they carry through life can serve as catalysts for greater change. For example, I work with many people impacted by addiction. When I ask clients if they would change the fact that they had addictions the resounding answer I hear is "no". People would shorten the amount of time they were in their active addictions (when they were self-destructing by drinking alcohol and/or drugging) and they would lessen the amount of pain they caused their families, but they would still wish to have addictions. For most individuals in recovery, addiction was the catalyst for tremendous personal growth as well as change. Many people find out what they are really made of as they grow into their true selves and then deepen their relationships with God. Also these same individuals are ready to walk through life with tremendous gratitude as well as appreciation because they do not have to live in the bondages of their old ways of thinking or escaping from the world with alcohol and/or drugs.

Addiction is one of the more identifiable problems as people suffer by losing their jobs as well as upsetting their families. With recovery, however, these same addicted people can heal as they experience incredible transformation in their lives as well as in the worlds of the people around them. Entire families can heal as well as transform from the negative impacts of addiction. Sometimes individuals have to descend into darkness in order to discover the true light that exists within their souls and in God's love. Therefore many people benefit from crashing and getting their emotional train-wrecks over with early in life so that they can get on with the emotional business of living in their full potentials. Thus the spiritual hurricane that God can facilitate is beneficial for not only particular individuals but for everyone involved.

Going Below The Iceberg

Not all of us as people are going to become saints from the adversity we suffer from in our lives and the pain that others create is difficult as well as heart-breaking. Often it is an enormous challenge to sees the positives or muster the courage to grow from these experiences. Pastor Peter Scazzero in his book *The Emotionally-Healthy Church* uses the metaphor of an iceberg to discuss how we as people can uses challenges in life as opportunities to go deeper to explore the depths of our interior worlds. In fact, Pastor Peter discusses how we can actually lead with brokenness as well as vulnerability in life. Sometimes we can be filled with pride, use judgements, or have such strong needs to please others that we do not grow on deeper emotional levels. Instead, we adjust our actions around what other people want us to be rather than doing the deeper, soul as well as authentic work to explore who we really are as we examine God's design for our lives. Psychologist Virginia Satir also used the iceberg metaphor as a way that we could explore our deeper values, principles, thoughts, feelings, and so on with the result being that we grow from our experiences. Pain in our lives is often a lesson in disguise. Once we learn from these situations, then we open up doorways to having new ways of being in this world. There are several lessons that we can learn from the pain of heartache in our lives. Remember that through crisis or the spiritual hurricanes in life that God is likely growing us to our higher purpose in this world and in order to be ready for these challenges we need to pioneer new aspects of ourselves.

Chapter 7
Stepping Into God's Larger Story

Christine stood on the stage of the church sharing with others her personal testimony of the power of God in her life. A few years ago she would have never imagined that she would be grateful for all of the struggles she had endured in her marriage. As she spoke further, she realized that many blessings from her life now stemmed from the deeper spiritual work she had completed during what she calls "the struggling years of her life." She welled with tears of gratitude around who she had now become and the valuable support she could offer to other people who were experiencing despair as well as hopelessness.

As people we can remain emotionally-stuck in life with the result being that we fall short of God's grace by not living up to the potential that God has for our lives. On the outside we may go through the motions of living as we obtain resources to feed as well as shelter our families as well as attend church to worship God. The problem is that on the inside some of us are not living to the full glory of God. Instead, we can be emotionally-disconnected from ourselves as well as others by being prideful, judgemental, or self-defeating in many ways. The result is that God can accelerate crisis or pre-existing problems that were created through our self-will or the self-will of others so that we are challenged to grow on deeper emotional levels. Therefore we can then return to God's glory and have a heart that is more loving as well as compassionate because we create healing in our own lives.

As mentioned, Peter Scazzerro wrote the book *The Emotionally-Healthy Church* and he outlines a number of principles for how we can go beneath the iceberg of who we are and resolve emotional issues that are holding us back from living a life of true greatness. An important part of returning to God's glory is to do the deeper spiritual work of exploring old thoughts, attitudes, ways of being, or approaches we have to relationships that do not serve us or God very well.

Pastor Peter Scazzerro states: "Without doing the work of becoming aware of your feelings and emotions, along with their impact on others it is scarcely possible to enter deeply into the life experiences of other people." (p.78) Therefore crisis in life is a very helpful moment for further deep reflection. During these moments "things are not going right" and we have the choice to blame others or we can use these experiences of pain as well as heartache in our relationships in order to grow on deeper emotional levels. We can remain fixated on what someone else did to us or we can take a profound look at the fact that we have inner faults or even unresolved emotional issues that are contributing to issues in our relationships. Even if our spouses were the ones who broke trust, this can become a time of deep reflection in our lives as we question who we are, why such problems happened, and so on during this time of intense confusion. The result is that we can grow into who we are meant to become and have even deeper or more fulfilling relationships with others and with God. When we grow from pain, we relinquish the barriers of ego that separate us from others.

I Didn't Mean For This To Happen

The ego is a protective part of ourselves that wants recognition, glory, and status. We can be easily wounded or offended by other people's words or we can remain in problematic relationships because it is too embarrassing or confronting to deal with our partner's emotional issues. Therefore we are guided in our interactions with others out of ego and not motivated by God's light and love. We do not rise to a higher good in our relationships because we do not honour our feelings and can sacrifice our integrity by ignoring issues in our relationships. Such actions are all part of acting out of ego and not connecting with our higher good or God's purpose for us in this world.

The Descent Into Ego

One way that we can remain emotionally-stuck in our relationships is that we believe that we are on the "assigned team of being right" or doing the correct things in life. We then surround ourselves with like-minded people who are similar to us. These people have the same ways of thinking or tackling situations in life. The difficulty is that we do not challenge our beliefs or ways of being in our relationships. Instead, we just do what we have always done and have learned from our original families while growing up. We can also not challenge ourselves on an emotional level because the people we surround ourselves with are focused on outside world activities or endeavours as well. For example, our homes are very important but our connections with others are around home decorating or other exterior world activities. Our attendance and connections at church may be around worshipping in God's love, but the difficulty is that we do not challenge ourselves on deeper emotional levels. We praise God for His greatness, but do not communicate around how we are really feeling. Instead, it can be easier to pretend that everything is good in our worlds as we sing about the glory of God. In fact, we may even believe that we look weak if we are struggling or that we are somehow less spiritual if we complain or feel emotionally challenged with different difficulties in our lives. Furthermore, we may even believe that we must uphold privacy in our worlds and we cannot let other people know that we are having difficulties or we will look weak or incapable as elders and leaders of the congregation.

In our interactions with other people, we may never be challenged to be ***authentic***. Our contacts are with others who depend on us for employment or we position ourselves as leaders so that individuals are always looking to us for guidance. We are supposed to come up with all the right answers in other people's lives without questioning the events or emotional details of our own lives. Some of us may even descend into ego as we grow on intellectual levels. We can sort through the issues in other people's worlds and use great analytical labels or descriptions to describe these situations. Meanwhile, we may even sever ourselves from our own deeper emotions. There are some us who might not even deal with emotional issues and would rather use outlets for escape which may include alcohol, fantasy obsession or pornography, compulsive spending, eating, or over-working, and so on. Then there are other individuals who are so emotionally-disconnected from other people that they are prideful and use judgements as well as comparisons to position themselves into a superior status. Such people are always looking at other people's faults or mistakes without questioning their own inner motivations or moral inventories.

Developing A Hardened Heart

When there are opportunities for deeper soul work and people come along who challenge us on deeper emotional levels, we may resist such spiritual transformation. For example, enemies or disagreeable people come along and rather than using these indi-

I Didn't Mean For This To Happen

viduals as gifts of learning in our lives we may feel wounded by their actions on an ego level. We may demonize others or be so focused on their faults or moral failings that we do not examine our own issues or question our own ways of dealing with situations. Remember we believe we are on the "good team" or are part of the people "who do things right." Therefore all other people who question or insult us are part of the group of individuals who need to grow up or have emotional issues. We may even label them as mood-disordered, crazy, or just plain irritating without examining why they are "pushing our own buttons" or making us upset. When individuals who are different from us question why we do something or do not agree with us, then they may be introducing a new way of thinking into our lives. Rather than embracing this learning, we might minimize or trivialize their thoughts and/or experiences. They are stupid, immature, or flawed in some way so we separate ourselves from them and keep them at an emotional arm's length distance away from our lives. Such people cause us irritation and they are nauseating because they drain our energies. In essence, we stop growing spiritually and instead our hearts become hardened.

What we may not realize is that the annoying people that God sends to us in our lives are part of a wake-up call that shows that the ways that we are dealing with life or approaching relationships may be self-defeating. Rather than looking at these experiences as learning opportunities, we may give ourselves honourable intentions and pray that these irritating individuals will learn the correct way of doing and being in life. As a result, we may heap more judgements on them and reinforce within ourselves our own positions of being right. In fact, we may even make it our personal mission to try to convince these individuals that their ways of thinking are not right as we attempt to rescue them or provide them with all kinds of advice.

We might not understand that these irritating individuals that God has provided are mirrors for us and what we see in their lives is a reflection of our own faults, shortcomings, or moral failings. As we progress in life, we may not continue to learn from our situations. Instead, we have used judgement, self-pride, pleasing, rescuing, or even plain denial as defences so that we do not have to grow on deeper interior levels. As a result, we remain in an emotional holding pattern so that the ways we are approaching life and our relationships may be self-defeating. How are we supposed to manifest the glory that God has created for our lives when we are living according to preserving our own egos? The result is that we do not grow or change and instead continue on "doing life" in the same ways without questioning that maybe the rules or ways of being that we have in life might be faulty.

Over time we can live with closed and hardened hearts as we try to position ourselves into greater status so we can be admired by others. As we enter church we may look good or be the envy of others because we appear to be a good family with righteous values. The problem is that we may have an emotional train-wreck in motion in our lives because we are acting in the ways we have always approached situations. We play roles and continue on doing the same things without ever questioning why we think or behave in certain ways. The irritating people that God has sent us have not got our attention. Instead, we minimize or trivialize all these individuals and do not use them as mirrors into our own souls. We find fault in them, without examining deeper our own characters. Therefore if God is to place His hand into our lives to grow us into who we are meant to be in this world, then we are challenged to pay attention to our flaws. As people God has a

I Didn't Mean For This To Happen

greater design for our lives and we must challenge ourselves to not fall short of His glory.

Refined Through Affliction

We are here to live from the heart that Jesus gave us and we cannot fully commit to God's work or will for our lives if we are trapped in ego. As a result, God accelerates the crisis occurring in our worlds and what better way to get our attention than to be impacted by broken trust in our marriages? When we have adversity in our relationships we may feel like our entire worlds are falling apart. Therefore we may question who we are, what has happened, and the role of God in our lives. As we pray that the pain be taken away, God unveils to us a different road that has much to do with not only our relationships but also our larger spiritual design as human beings. God is sculpting our souls for His work in this world and through pain we become ready to follow His will. We are like silver that is refined by fire except that we are tempered through the affliction of our lives (Isaiah 48:10).We have the choice to wallow in the pain as well as confusion of our experiences or to get on with the business of growing on deeper spiritual levels. In fact, our entire ideas of who we are and what we want for our lives may even be brought into question as our marriages move into crisis. We as people may need to hit our emotional bottoms in life as we realize that our hearts have become closed as well as hardened and that God's image for who we are supposed to become is not properly reflected. Thus, God brings to light through crisis and pain parts of ourselves we may have not even realized. Suddenly, with adversity, we may learn to appreciate aspects of our personalities or inner strengths that we may have not even acknowledged or fulfilled. Essentially, we can be off track for the will that God has in our lives and the crisis we endure is a signal to re-align with God's greater will for our spiritual souls. We may have believed we were supposed to be walking along a certain path only to realize we are meant to cross a bridge and move in another direction which will bring us to a land we could have never in our wildest dreams imagined. This is a world with true blessings as we live in the light of Jesus and in the fullest potential of our lives. We become changed by our experiences and with crisis things in life cannot be the same. Our choice is whether the change in ourselves and in life will be negative or positive.

It is with chaos as well as confusion that we can be called into God's greater plans for our worlds. When we receive a large dose of what we do not want in life through problems then we can realize the personal limitations that we may have placed on ourselves. In crisis we focus on what is really important in life and suddenly we may understand that we have been blown off course as well as direction. We may not be living an authentic life true to ourselves. Now with God's hand in our lives we can grow through these experiences and perhaps even reach deeper levels of healing individually or as a couple. In fact, we may now be living a relationship whereby God is truly at the center of our lives. Each day we can pray for knowledge of His will for us. Now as we walk through life with a sense of humility we can open our hearts to truly connecting with others rather than positioning ourselves as superior with our judgements. God has not abandoned us and has instead held our hands to gently lead us back to our real homes where he is at the center of our lives and we are returning to His glory!

Chapter 8
Live The Choice Now!

I am going to give you a challenge that I will call the "One Year Place Challenge." Should you accept this mission, then you are committing to being in a better emotional place or healthiness in a year from now. This is much like drawing a start line through the center of your life as part of a "fresh start" or new beginning. What this means is that you are going to deal with an emotional issue in your life and finally put this problem to rest. Along your spiritual path you have encountered an emotional boulder which is a problem blocking your way to full happiness. You may feel like this boulder or obstruction is insurmountable and you can't possibly imagine how you are going to get over it, around it, and with the weight of this burden you most certainly cannot crawl under it. So there you are...stuck, defeated, fearful, and probably exhausted at the possibility of moving this boulder or problem out of your way.

The mystery that you do not know is that the emotional boulder before you is actually a pebble. What if you had the perspective to see your way around the boulder and had the energy to raise your leg high in the air to step over this obstacle? In fact, the issue is one of perspective so that you see the burdensome emotional boulder as the pebble that it actually is in this world. With emotional fitness, you have the energy, knowledge, and skills to "power up" for any challenge in your life. This means having the ability to reduce emotional boulders into pebbles in your world.

So let's begin this work! Your "One Year Place Challenge" begins right now! Three quarters of the work is identifying what you are even dealing with as an issue. Often we are reacting and feel like we are sliding out of control in our issues. By gaining perspective we figure out exactly what it is we are dealing with in the first place.

Step #1: Figure Out Why And How You "Lost Your Inner Happy."

This is the shadow of the emotional boulder or obstacle in your life. Your opportunity is to figure out exactly what is bugging you and why you are so unhappy right now? That natural joy within yourself is fading, hidden, or has been dampened like smothered coals in a furnace. What happened and how did you lose "your inner happy?" Yes, we have taken the word "happy" and turned it into a noun because it is a thing, an experience, a natural part of who you are living inside of you. God wants us to be happy so we know that the Lord wants us to live life to the fullest (John 10:10) and that He has plans to prosper us (Jeremiah 29:11). But, somewhere along the way you lost, gave away, or sold out your "happy" to someone else or a situation in your life.

Step #2: Identify The Thief

At this moment, your opportunity is to identify the thief or thieves (there may be more than one) that are stealing your "inner happy." This is the source of the shadow in your life. Why is the light of happiness and joy being overshadowed in your world? What is stealing your happiness? Chances are that you are allowing the thief of fear into your world and this thief is stealing, pillaging, and reeking havoc all over your inner emotional world!

So let's call out the two most common thieves into the light of God for healing.

Thief #1- "If Only Happiness"

I Didn't Mean For This To Happen

We believe we can be happy "if only" someone else would change or do what it is that we expect them to do. If a situation would work out in a particular way, then we think we will be happy. Therefore with fear we try and manage outcomes and people in order to achieve certain results which we think will make us happy. What we do not realize is that happiness is not something outside of ourselves and is not dependent on what people are doing or how situations are working out in our lives. Instead, happiness is a state within ourselves that can be an ongoing peace in our connection with the Lord that is independent of what is occurring in our outer worlds. When we step into the covering of God's grace and connect to the Lord we trust that there is a larger story and we hand the details as well as burdens in our lives to God for healing. We stop, listen, and figure out His will of where we are going and what this all means right now!

Thief #2- "What If Overwhelm"

As people we live in two realities which includes the reality of what is happening right now and what we know for sure to be occurring. The other reality is the "what if", fear-based reality of "what could" happen in our worlds. Many of us as people are afraid to "let our guards down" and allow joy into our lives because we are worried that something bad will happen so we are prepared as we brace for another negative episode or anticipate how our greatest fears may come true. If we are ready, then we think the sting of such pain will not feel so bad when it arrives. Instead, with a negative state of mind we feel ready for the bad things to occur in our lives. If we are already anticipating disappointment, then when the disappointment arrives it won't be that bad...right? Or even worse some people delude themselves into believing that they are actually "warding off" bad things from happening as they play out their greatest fears in their minds. Such individuals believe that getting themselves "all worked up" is a way of averting bad things from happening. As a result, the "what if overwhelm" thief rushes in and takes charge of our inner worlds causing us to live in constant fear as well as anxiety!

So now you have the chance to identify the thieves of happiness in your emotional world. What is stealing your "inner happy?"

Congratulations! You have completed three quarters of the journey and a year is not even up! Maybe only a few minutes have gone by. Yes, it is that simple. Now you have gained back perspective. You are handing your happiness over to thieves who are creating chaos and a fear-based reality in your inner emotional world. When you step out of the fear, you see that the emotional boulder or obstacle in front of you is actually a pebble.

The challenge now is to maintain that perspective and this is a choice that you have a chance to live each day!

Step #3: Live The Choice Now!

You have the opportunity to "step into the worthiness" of happiness and joy in your life. This may sound strange but you actually have to give yourself permission to be happy or to reclaim back your life from fear and negativity. It is so much easier to be fearful, upset, and negative than to take the risk of being happy (letting your guard down) only to have something bad happen later. Therefore many people skip the process of allowing themselves to be happy because it is easier to just attach to all the bad stuff and get the pain over with in the meantime. Many individuals have an illusion of control if they work themselves into a state of fear or negativity. No one can make them feel bad because they have done it to themselves first!

How we feel comes from our thoughts. In fact our thoughts lead to our emotions which then result in our actions. If we want

I Didn't Mean For This To Happen

to change our reality, we must first address our thoughts and hold them up for examination. In fact, if we live a life whereby we are waiting for people to change or for situations to turn out in our favor, then we will be sadly disappointed. Our sense of "happy" will be outside of ourselves and we will live on an emotional rollercoaster of highs and lows rebounding off of situations, people, places, and things according to our expectations and our wills.

The opportunity is to "get our happy back" and "protect our happy" as we reclaim our lives back from negativity as well as fear. We allow people to have their own issues and their emotional process while focusing on ourselves and our healthiness. This means that we walk alongside people who are having issues but we allow them to "carry their own emotional backpacks" while becoming clear around our own "emotional back packs in life." As a result, we focus on our own issues and personal healthiness without collapsing under the weight of our own backpacks and those packs of everyone around us.

In the simplest terms, we make a commitment to be okay inside of ourselves even if things around us in our outer worlds are not okay at the moment. We do not pin our sense of happiness on externals (people/places/things outside of us.) Viktor Frankl in *Man's Search For Meaning* is a classic example of how as people one of our last human freedoms is where we place our minds. As a Psychiatrist trapped in Nazi concentration camps, Viktor Frankl showed us that we have a choice of how to think and that in spite of absolute human horror we have control over our thoughts around how to survive as well as maintain our inner emotional balance no matter what is occurring externally around us.

The problem is that many of us spiral in fear as well as negativity and we forget that we have a choice. In essence, we lose perspective and the pebbles in our worlds start becoming emotional boulders. We do not use our skills of *emotional fitness* and some of us may even distance ourselves from God in resentment because we feel that He is allowing bad things to happen to us.

In order to *live the choice now* we make the commitment to reclaim back our "inner happy." We remember that we have the choice and we actively keep the "thieves" at bay so that we do not hand over our inner peace to negativity.

The problem is that negativity and unhealthy or fear-based thinking builds up within our minds like a fog. We will call this the "fog of unhealthy thinking." When we are in the fog of fear, fog of addiction, or impaired thinking of any kind then we cannot see our way out of our situations. We forget we have a choice and we just continue on reacting in our old ways of doing things.

The challenge then is to "get out of our minds" and to get some perspective. This clarity comes with reaching out and connecting to something greater than ourselves. Furthermore, we are healthiest in community so when we take the time to connect with others through conversation, attend bible study groups, rigorously spend time alone with the Lord in devotion as well as prayer, and so forth then we create the emotional space as well as time to "get out of our heads" and into the light of God and His will. We stop panicking in fear and the volume of noise in our minds of thoughts slows down as we develop clarity around our direction or path according to God's larger design for our lives.

CPA Recovery System

One way of keeping the fog of unhealthy thinking at bay and to manage the motivation to *live the choice now* by staying healthy is to build a support system. This means:

a) Creating a positive action or a commitment to positive action (CPA). What will you do to stay emotionally healthy?

I Didn't Mean For This To Happen

b) Take an on-line course to learn about why/how you slip into old patterns of unhealthy thinking. Why do you lose yourself in the unhealthiness of others or why does stress get to you so much? Look at the selection of on-line courses at www.reallifetoolbox.com

c) Choose an accountability partner or someone you can talk to who will keep you motivated to stay on track with the healthy decisions in your life. Accountability partner training courses are available at www.reallife-toolbox.com

d) Choose an accountability system. What do you need to "gatekeep" or what triggers do you need to eliminate from your life so that you stay on track for being healthy?

e) Join an accountability community. Attend a bible study group or join an on-line POD Tutorial group (visit www.reallifetoolbox.com for some options) so that you meet regularly on-line to talk about how to stay on track with healthy and positive thinking so that you can always be in your greatest potential in life by living out God's calling for yourself.

If You Feel Like You Are Sliding

Positive thinking, the motivation to change in healthy ways, and so forth is a regular as well as daily choice. With fear and negative thinking patterns we lose perspective and forget that we have choices. This is part of a process that is not always easy. Often we will slip back into old ways of thinking and the thieves of happiness will rush back into our lives as we become overwhelmed with fear and start losing perspective. We do not "arrive" at being happy or finding inner serenity. Instead, this is part of a process and requires intentional as well as active work each day. Just like with a physical fitness program or regime we maintain our weight as well as health goals, with *emotional fitness* we need daily healthy habits, resources, and a support system. Our opportunity each day is to *live the choice now* by stepping into healthiness.

Now you may feel like the fog of overwhelm will come back into your life or that the negative thinking patterns are beginning to pile up in your mind. Someone may do something or say something that "sends you over the edge" whereby you feel out of control and upset again. If you decide to *live the choice now*, then you will have to actively "unhook" from these people or situations to get yourself back again. In situations whereby you are extremely upset you are giving people the "power to light you up" or throw you off-balance. In many ways you may be like a "Christmas tree" lighting up in reaction to someone else you have given your personal power away to in a negative interaction. Like bulbs on a Christmas tree you are lit up and are powering or fuelling a situation. Unfortunately, being lit up like a Christmas tree in negative situations is not a good thing! In the end you are overcharged and have expended so much emotional energy that you feel burned out.

If you **live the choice now**, you acknowledge that you are giving other people the "power to light you up." Now you have an opportunity to see what fears are being activated in yourself. This is a challenge for you to grow.

Below are some exercises:
a) Acknowledge you are "lit up."
b) Explore why this person is "getting under your skin", upsetting you, or having the "power to light you up." What fear are they activating within you? How are the thieves of happiness rushing in to take control?

I Didn't Mean For This To Happen

c) Take a piece of paper and draw a line down the center of the page titled healthy (new way) and unhealthy (old way). Write how you could react in an unhealthy way to being "lit up." Then write down how you will react if you are to respond in a healthy way. When you **live the choice now** you have an opportunity to draw a new start line through the center of your life. Furthermore, you have the chance to "step into a healthy response." Each new day there is a new way. You can choose happiness by actively as well as intentionally giving yourself permission to be healthy.

So What Does This All Look Like?

This book has served as an emotional compass pointing you in a particular direction along a journey in which you take negative experiences in life around broken trust and grow from them as you move a step closer towards your greatest potential as well as God's overall design for your life. While reading this book, we have identified some important tools, skills, and milestones that you are heading in the right direction of your journey. As many people acquire these skills they want to know what this journey actually looks like in day to day life. Individuals do not "arrive" at healthiness and it is with daily intentional work and thought along with the creation of new habits they start to make significant positive changes in their relationships as well as emotional worlds. So let's look at what this journey is like in one couple's life which we will call Doug and Donna.

Doug and Donna are a couple in their forties with three children who are all in their teens. For years Doug has been struggling with lusting and he is "overly familiar" with the female friends and acquaintances that are part of their life. Doug also has issues with pornography which he "dabbles in" watching from time to time but the source of trust issues really come from his flirtations with other women in front of Donna. As a result, Donna feels humiliated as well as devalued. She is very frustrated with Doug because he tells her that she is overreacting and has a jealous personality. This has been an ongoing issue in the marriage until one day Donna intercepted a very inappropriate e-mail between Doug and another lady in a different part of the United States. They were having cybersex and Doug was describing his sexual fantasy world to this woman on-line via e-mails. Of course Donna was devastated and with all the years of pent up frustration she feels extreme rage which she thinks she cannot express without Doug getting upset so she turns this anger inwards as she manifests these angry feelings into depression. Donna then crashes into bed and has found comfort in food as she "emotionally eats" away her problems. She is rapidly gaining weight and her level of self-loathing is increasing daily. Now with the interception of this e-mail, Donna feels like she is on the verge of a nervous breakdown.

So where do they start?

First of all, Donna can *live the choice now*. The emotional boulder in her life is the trust issue with Doug which then results in depression as well as emotional-eating. Donna is beginning to shut-off and shut-down from life which is impacting her relationship with her kids significantly as well. Donna can wait for Doug to make a change but if she waits for him to get healthy and recognize the errors of his ways, then she is handing her serenity to the "If Only Happiness" thief and her life will get better "if only" Doug would stop acting-out. The reality is that if Donna gets healthy herself, then poor treatment from Doug will no longer feel comfortable. If Donna starts to work on her emotional fitness and develop her core confidence then she will start to grow into healthy responses as she raises her value in this relationship.

I Didn't Mean For This To Happen

Doug then has a choice to come and "meet her in her value" by addressing his unhealthy behaviours or he will struggle with positive change. This is Doug's choice but what we know for sure is that the dynamics in the relationship will not stay the same if one person starts to grow into healthiness. Relationships are much like a dance and if one partner shifts up the dance steps into healthiness then the other partner has to respond in some way. The old unhealthy dance is no longer at play.

So Donna takes the "one year place challenge" and draws a new start line through the center of her life regardless of what Doug does or does not do. As a result, Donna realizes she has a choice and begins her healing journey. Donna identifies the issue which is one of trust and sees how the thieves of happiness are stealing joy from her life. She begins a process of reclaiming her life back from fear and negativity as she commits to growing as a better person from this negative experience in her life.

Now Donna's emotional world is beginning to open up. As a result of *living the choice now*, Donna draws a line between unhealthy and healthy reactions. In an unhealthy way she can continue to eat away her problems and shut-down from life. With a healthy way, she will challenge herself to learn a new toolbox of skills for how to deal with issues in her life as well as her relationship.

Now Donna has options as she can:

-Make a commitment to positive change (CPA). Her commitment is to get herself back because she feels like she is losing herself in Doug's unhealthy acting-out issues. She is going to reclaim her life back from negativity as well as fear.

-Donna can work through *Core-Confidence: Stepping Into Your Greatest Potential-Stepping Into Your Greatest Life Workbook* as she learns about how to get herself back again and develop the confidence to deal with the issues in her marriage while also finding herself again as she explores who she really is and grows into God's calling for her life. She makes a commitment to becoming healthy within herself rather than rebounding off of Doug's issues or living in the constant oppression as well as fear that Doug is going to "cheat on her" with another woman or that his eyes are wandering elsewhere.

-Donna can take an on-line course and begin creating a toolbox of skills for how to deal with communication and stand up to face the issues in her marriage. There is a selection of courses from www.reallifetoolbox.com that she can choose from as she begins her journey.

For example some on-line courses include:

a) **Core Confidence** (a free 4 week on-line course to learn how to increase emotional fitness and deal with problems or issues in your life.)

b) **Reclaiming Your Life-** (a forty-eight week on-line program to learn about how to heal yourself from the impact of someone else's acting-out and the resulting trust issues in your relationship)

c) **Boundaries** (an eight week on-line course on how to learn to set healthy limits in relationships)

d) **I Don't Trust You: How To Confront Someone Around Broken Trust And Begin The Healing** (a four week on-line course on how to deal with and talk about an issue of trust in a marriage.) Donna may want to take this course in particular to learn some tools or skills around how to deal with the e-mail issue she

I Didn't Mean For This To Happen

found where Doug was sending an inappropriate sexual e-mail to another woman.

e) **How To Communicate With Someone Who Doesn't Communicate** (a four week on-line course around how to deal with a spouse who has issues with communication).

f) **Emotional Eating: Normal, Compulsion or Addiction?** (a four week on-line course to learn about the pattern of emotional eating and how to deal with underlying issues which are driving the over-eating behaviour.) Donna can learn the difference between physical and emotional hunger as she focuses on how to work through her issues of eating away uncomfortable feelings.

-Donna can work out a plan around how she will continue with her positive changes within herself by completing a core confidence or care plan with an on-line wellness coach through www.reallifetoolbox.com

-Donna can keep this commitment to positive action (CPA) going by getting a support system of accountability partners who she checks in with to talk about how she is feeling. If these people wanted training in how to be an accountability partner they could take the accountability partner training on-line course at www.reallifetoolbox.com

-Donna can get together with other women who are dealing with similar struggles and join at POD Tutorial which is like a cyberspace support group and these sessions are led by an on-line wellness coach at www.reallifetoolbox.com

-Donna can do devotionals each day and as part of her prayer time with God, she can do a journal entry in her "From Fear To Faith" journal. More details are available at www.livethechoicenow.com

Donna is participating in these positive changes within herself and now Doug can join her in this healing journey. Doug has a variety of supports that he can explore as well.

Some options for Doug on-line skills for living classes at www.reallifetoolbox.com which include:

a) **Finding Freedom** (a forty-eight week on-line program for people who are struggling with acting-out behaviours, self-destructive patterns, and/or addictions as they learn about recovery.)

b) **The Road To Healing From Pornography** (a four week on-line program for people who are struggling with pornography and want to begin recovery from these issues.)

c) **Sex: Normal, Compulsion, or Addiction** (a four week on-line program for people wanting to learn about sexual acting-out and sexual addiction as well as how to start recovery on these issues.)

d) **Self-Sabotage: Why When Things Are Going Well Do I Mess Them Up?** (a four week on-line program for people who experience good things happening in life and then manage to sabotage this success by acting-out or self-destructing in ways that cause themselves further problems. In this course participants learn about patterns of self-sabotage and how to change these patterns.)

e) **I Have A Secret: How To Talk About The Trust You Have Broken And Then Begin The Healing** (a four week on-line program for people who have been hiding secrets in their relationships and how to deal with these issues in a positive way rather than living with constant guilt and further deception.)

I Didn't Mean For This To Happen

-Doug may also want to work with an on-line wellness coach on an *accountability and recovery plan* to manage his lusting and sort out how to be healthy in his marriage.

-Doug can join a group of people who are struggling with similar issues through on-line POD Tutorial support which is like a cyberspace support group and these sessions are led by an on-line wellness coach.

Together Doug and Donna may want to explore couple's supports which include:

a) **New Horizons** (a forty-eight week on-line course for couples wanting to rebuild their relationships after trust has been broken as they begin healing these issues.)

b) **Communication** (an eight week on-line course for couples wanting to work on building healthy communication in their relationships.)

c) **Keeping The Connection** (a four week on-line course for couples wanting to increase intimacy in their relationships.)

d) **Healing Resentments** (a four week on-line course for couples wanting to rebuild trust and overcome resentments in their relationships.)

e) **Healthy Sex and Sexuality For Married Couples** (a six week on-line course for couples wanting to connect in deeper emotional as well as physical intimacy with each other as they learn about how to enhance their sexual health in the relationship.)

-Doug and Donna can also work out a plan around how they will keep going with their positive changes by completing a *couple's north star plan* with an on-line wellness coach through www.reallifetoolbox.com

Now Doug and Donna do not have to do everything listed above as they are on a healing journey from their issues. The resources above are part of a smorgasbord of options and ultimately Doug and Donna have to decide for themselves what resources are going to be helpful but if they decide to *live the choice now* they can then open up their emotional worlds and see that there are options as they begin an exciting new healing journey by retiring the old self-destructive patterns of the past.

Live The Choice Now!
One Year Place Challenge
A New Start Line To Healthy!

Each day I make the choice of where to place my mind and my thoughts. I can place my mind into the sea of fear as the waves of stress sweep me into further turmoil. The negativity can consume my soul or I can take a step out of the abyss for even a moment. My choice is to step into the positive. As I draw a new start line to healthy each day I reclaim my life back from negativity as well as fear. I live the choice now as I step out from the shadows and darkness of fear into the light of God's healing. When I embrace this choice my world opens up and I cross the line from "what if fears" to "what could be…potential" as I can now see opportunities as I move from fear into faith. I see what God wants me to see as I embrace my potential, my light, and the Lord's greatest direction. As a result, my world changes because each day I live the choice!

I take the "one year place challenge" knowing that in a year from now as I live the choice each day, I can be in a better as well as stronger emotional place in my life. I live the choice now by making the commitment to be positive and healthy.

References

-Frankl, Viktor (2006). *Man's Search For Meaning*. USA: Beacon Press

-Scazzero, Peter (2010). *The Emotionally-Healthy Church: A Strategy For Discipleship That Actually Changes Lives*. USA: Zondervan

Another Book By Cathy Patterson-Sterling...

-*Core Confidence: Stepping Into Your Greatest Potential-Stepping Into Your Greatest Life* (2012). Available at www.amazon.com

We all have a higher purpose for our lives and a larger calling through the design as well as will of God. Do you know your calling? More importantly, are you afraid of this calling and is part of your confusion based out of fear?

Many people are their own worst enemies as they are held back from reaching their goals or even connecting with God's higher purpose or calling for their lives because of their fears around disappointing others, worries about what other people think, and their needs around living for the approval of others. Such individuals live with the shadow of insecurity of people-pleasing which looms over their lives as they end up coasting through this world rebounding like an emotional yo-yo off of what other people think they should do or not. In this book, readers will learn how to stop patterns of people-pleasing as they develop the necessary skills of resiliency and emotional fitness. By learning these secrets of how to develop internal strength, a solid emotional core, and a deep sense of core confidence, readers can learn to "power up" for any challenge in life. Much like how we have physical fitness with muscular as well as cardio endurance, we also have emotional as well as spiritual fitness as we develop the inner resiliency and confidence to charter our course towards our destinies as we grow into the greatest potential of our lives.

*For more information visit www.livethechoicenow.com

Made in the USA
Coppell, TX
01 July 2023